liberating the soul

A GUIDE FOR SPIRITUAL GROWTH
volume three

By

Shaykh Nazim Adil Al-Haqqani

Foreword By
Shaykh Muhammad Hisham Kabbani

ISLAMIC SUPREME COUNCIL OF AMERICA

Library of Congress Cataloging-in-Publication Data

Naqshbandi, Muhammad Nazim Adil al-Haqqani, 1922-
Liberating the soul : a guide for spiritual growth / by Shaykh Nazim Adil al-Haqqani.
1ˢᵗ ed.
Washington, DC : Islamic Supreme Council of America, <2002-2005 >
v. <1-3> ; 23 cm.

Subjects: Sufism. Naqshaband‾iyah.
Series: Sufi wisdom series
BP189 .N368 2002 297.4 21

2002109747

Published and Distributed by:
Islamic Supreme Council of America

17195 Silver Parkway, #401

Fenton, MI 48430 USA
Tel: (888) 278-6624

Fax:(810) 815-0518
Email: staff@naqshbandi.org
Web: http://www.naqshbandi.org

First Edition July 2005
ISBN: 1-930409-16-8

Shaykh Nazim Adil al-Haqqani (right) with his disciple of fifty years, Shaykh Muhammad Hisham Kabbani. Head of the world's largest Naqshbandi Sufi spiritual order, Shaykh Nazim is known for his life-altering lessons in how to discipline the ego, reach a state of spiritual surrender, and achieve true liberation from the bondage of worldly distraction and pursuit. Shaykh Hisham Kabbani, Shaykh Nazim's deputy, accompanies the venerable shaykh on his many visits to various regions of the world, where they meet with political and religious leaders, media, and throngs of common folk.

table of contents

foreword

Bismillahi-r-Rahmani-r-Rahim
In the Name of Allah, the Most Beneficent, the Most Merciful

All praise is due to God Almighty, Allah the Exalted and Bounteous. And praise and blessings be upon His perfect servant, the exemplar to humankind and mercy to all creation, Prophet Muhammad ﷺ,[1] and on his family and Companions.

This third in the series, *Liberating the Soul,* is another wonderful compendium of *sohbets* or spiritual discourses by our master, the chief of saints and reviver of the prophetic way, the *Sunnah,* in an age of gross materialism; the teacher of millions and worldwide leader of the Naqshbandi-Haqqani Sufi Order, Mawlana Shaykh Muhammad Nazim Adil al-Haqqani, may Allah grant him bountiful health and a long life.

In this time, true saints are rare. But gnostics, knowers of divine realities, *al-'arifin bil-Lah,* are still more rare. Indeed, they are scarce to the point of being non-existent.

The Last Prophet, Sayyidina Muhammad ﷺ, was the humblest of creation, and when one is humble, he will be granted spiritual knowledge. But those who are arrogant and filled with pride will be discarded in the manner of those who recite from books like a parrot but without spirit or soul, having neither sweetness nor taste, merely repeating letters that are collected together, which is nothing more than 'the knowledge of papers,' *'ilm al-awraq.*

---

[1] ﷺ stands for *"Salla-Lahu 'alayhi wa sallam,"* meaning, "Allah's peace and blessings be upon him," the Islamic invocation for Prophet Muhammad.

The archangel Gabriel ﷺ commanded Prophet Muhammad ﷺ to read. Despite the fact that the Prophet ﷺ was unlettered *(umiyyun)*, not knowing how to handle a pen, nonetheless Allah ordered him three times through the angel, "Read!" The secret of this is contained in the second repetition of the order: *"Read, and your Lord is Most Generous, who taught by means of the pen—taught the human being what he did not know"* (Qur'an, 96:3-5).

Thus, like Prophet Muhammad ﷺ, the *'arif bi-Llah*, the gnostic, does not learn by means of letters, for although he may read and write, he is 'unlettered'. Rather than learning from books, his teacher pours into his heart the interpretation and the secrets behind the letters, so that he will begin to extract meanings that others are unable to extract. From such meanings comes a sweetness and taste that cannot be attained in any other way. That taste, *dhawq*, comes from "the knowledge of taste," *'ilm al-adhwaq*, not the knowledge of "he said, she said," the mere written word. And all of it is achieved through humbleness.

The renowned North African saint al-Hasan ibn al-Mansour said:

> The identity of God's elect servant becomes extinguished in the Divine Presence. No one bears such a person, nor does that person put up with [standards of behavior] that others tolerate. Yet the elected one among God's servants is like the earth: it accepts every type of refuse and yet nothing issues from it but sweetness. Both the good and the sinner walk over and tread upon the servant of God.

The early Iraqi saint *(wali-Ullah)* ash-Shibli said, "The elect servant of God is cut off from creatures and connected to Truth."[3]

Ibn 'Ajiba, another North African *wali-Ullah*, relates that it has been said, "Whoever possesses states whose character indicates closeness to God

---

[2] ﷺ stands for *"'Alayhi/'Alayha-s-salam,"* the Islamic invocation for angels, prophets other than Muhammad, and certain holy personages such as Sayyidina Khidr, the blessed Virgin Mary and the Mahdi.

[3] From *The Commentary of the Hikam of Ibn Ataillah as-Sakandari* by Ibn Ajiba *(Ikaz al-himmam fi sharhi-l-hikam li Ahmad bin Muhammad bin Ajiba al-Hasani*, p. 4).

is insupportable. The mountains cannot carry him." Such is the aspect of one who realizes the station of extinction, *maqam al-fana*.[4]

Al-Hasan ibn al-Mansour said of the one who became extinguished *(fani)* in the love of God:

> People find it difficult to tolerate the one who has lost any sense of self and who stands in awe, stunned before Allah's Absolute Existence. The one who reaches that station *[maqam]* and would in any way divulge its secret will [necessarily] act differently from the commonality of humankind.

For that reason, the Friends of God *(awliya-Llah)*[5] who reach that station hide themselves. The story of al-Khidr 🕊 in the Holy Qur'an illustrates this truth.[6] Khidr 🕊 did things that people normally do not do, things that even the Prophet Moses 🕊 found difficult to accept. Allah instructs us by means of that example to learn—and not because Moses 🕊 is lower in station, for he is after all one of the five greatest prophets in Islam, and no one can attain the level of the prophets and of the Prophet's Companions *(sahabah)*. But by informing us of the prophet Moses' 🕊 relationship to Khidr 🕊, Allah intends to give us the example of one brought near to Him, one of His saints. Such individuals are just as the holy *hadith*[7] describes them: "My saints are under My domes; no one knows them except Me." Allah Himself hides His saints, since they are exceedingly precious to Him. Another *hadith*, "Whoever comes against a Friend of Mine, I declare war on him,"[8] underscores the tremendous value Allah gives to his saints.

In the midst of people, the Friends of Allah may sometimes say or do things that others do not accept. That is the meaning of Ibn Ajiba's words, "No one can carry such a person." Thus it was that when the Prophet, Sayyid-

---

[4]*Maqam*: what a servant of Allah realizes in his station in terms of spiritually-perfected manners, *adab*, and what is communicated. (Al-Qushayri)

[5]Singular, *wali*; literally, "friend of God."

[6]See Holy Qur'an, (18:60–82)

[7]That is, a *qudsi hadith*, a sacred *hadith* in which Allah Most High speaks about Himself by divine inspiration through the tongue of His Prophet 🕊.

[8]Even the rigorous Ibn Taymiyya verified this *hadith*.

ina Muhammad ﷺ, stood up and called his people to the Oneness of God Almighty, Allah, his people rejected him, as other prophets before him had been rejected by their people. And since this was the case with the prophets, what can be expected for saints, *awliya*? It is only natural that they will be rejected by common people, who see them as ordinary human beings, never understanding that Allah Himself has bestowed upon them heavenly power.

Today's religious scholars *('ulama)* say that there no longer remain any such Friends of Allah, *awliya-Llah*. But this is not true. Rather, such scholars of the external have become so blind that they cannot see them and the Friends of Allah have hidden themselves, especially in the present era. They know that virtually no one will accept them and the power granted them by their Lord. If they display anything of that with which they have been empowered, people will come against them.

Thus, the highest level of saint, *wali*, is one who acts like an ordinary person and does not appear different from others in aspect or behavior. Indeed, a Friend of Allah may behave like others to the extent that people say about him, "He is like us. What's different?" What they do not know about him is that he has been tested by *awliya*, by the Prophet ﷺ, and finally by Allah the Exalted, and that he has passed his tests and been given his spiritual trusts *(amanat)*.

Mawlana Shaykh Nazim is one such gnostic. We have truly been fortunate to be able to sit at his feet and to learn, and with his permission to spread the light of his teachings east and west, north and south. Seekers circle the flame of his spiritual light and seek to quench their thirst at the bounteous fountain of his wisdom, which flows unceasingly from his heart

There is fresh fruit and there is plastic fruit. Real fruit has a taste such that when you eat it, its essence is experienced. Plastic fruit has no taste; it has only the appearance of fruit. In like manner, the knowledge and teaching of a shaykh who has been authorized through a chain of saints going back to the Prophet ﷺ will be flavorful. Understandings and realities will appear to that shaykh from the Beautiful Names and Attributes of Allah, *Asmullahu-l-Husna*, and from his teachings the listener or reader will be clothed in something of the secrets of these Names. Allah will bestow His mercy and His manifestations on such a person when he is reading the shaykh's words because in doing so, whether he is aware of it or not, he is connected through his heart, through the shaykh to his grandshaykh, and so on up to Sayyidina Abu Bakr as-Siddiq ⚘,[9] and from Sayyidina Abu Bakr to the Prophet ⚘.

The secret Shaykh Nazim carries is a manifestation of Allah's tremendous love and mercy to him. Allah has authorized him with that power and authority because he has maintained inimitable sincerity, piety and loyalty to Allah's religion, held fast to every obligation, and honored the Holy Qur'an and the Prophet's *Sunnah* with the highest respect. He is like all the saints of the Naqshbandi Order and the saints of other orders before him—like his forefathers Sayyidina 'Abdul Qadir Jilani and Sayyidina Jalaluddin Rumi, and like Muhyideen Ibn 'Arabi, who followed and preserved the traditions of Islam for 1400 years.

Therefore, approach this book with reverence, for it contains precious jewels of guidance and understanding. Know that the words of the gnostics are special. One may read them, reread them and reread them yet again, and each time they give a fresh taste and a new understanding. For this reason, it is said that the words of the gnostics never grow stale. Mawlana Shaykh Nazim's teachings exemplify this characteristic, for if anyone in difficulty or seeking good counsel picks up a volume of his *sohbets*, immediately, upon opening it to any page, seeking to address the problem at hand, he or she will find the solace and guidance appropriate to the problem at that moment. Hence, among the saints, Shaykh Nazim is considered *Sahib al-Waqt*, "the Man of the Time," and his teachings are comprehensive, inspiring and appropriate for the people of this time and their conditions.

We humbly present this volume to you as a source of blessing and wisdom.

Shaykh Muhammad Hisham Kabbani
Fenton, Michigan
February 12, 2005

---

[9] ⚘ stands for *"Radi-Allahu 'anhu/anha,"* the Islamic invocation for the male/female Companions of the Prophet.

introduction

Endless praise and thanks be to God Most High, who guides His servants to His light by means of other servants of His whose hearts He illuminates with His divine love.

Since the beginning of human history, God Most High has conveyed His revealed guidance to mankind through His prophets and messengers, beginning with the first man, Adam ﷺ. The prophetic line includes such well-known names as Noah, Abraham, Ishmael, Isaac, Jacob, Joseph, Lot, Moses, David, Solomon, and Jesus, peace be upon them all, ending and culminating in Muhammad, the Seal of the Prophets ﷺ, a descendant of Abraham, who brought the final revelation from God to all mankind.

But although there are no longer prophets upon the earth, the Most Merciful Lord has not left His servants without inspired teachers and guides. *Awliya*—holy people or saints—are the inheritors of the prophets. Up to the Last Day, these "friends of God," the radiant beacons of truth, righteousness and the highest spirituality, will continue in the footsteps of the prophets, calling people to their Lord and guiding seekers to His glorious Divine Presence.

One such inspired teacher, a shaykh or *murshid* of the Naqshbandi Sufi Order, is Shaykh Nazim Adil al-Qubrusi al-Haqqani. A descendant not only of the holy prophet Muhammad ﷺ but also of the great Sufi masters 'Abul Qadir Gilani and Jalaluddin Rumi, Shaykh Nazim was born in Larnaca, Cyprus, in 1922 during the period of British rule of the island. Gifted from earliest childhood with an extraordinarily spiritual personality, Shaykh Nazim received his spiritual training in Damascus at the hands of Maulana Shaykh 'Abdullah ad-Daghestani (fondly referred to as "Grandshaykh"), the mentor of such well-known figures as Gurjieff and J. G. Bennett, over a period of forty years.

Before leaving this life in 1973, Grandshaykh designated Shaykh Nazim as his successor. In 1974, Shaykh Nazim went to London for the first time, thus initiating what was to become a yearly practice during the month of Ramadan up to 1990s. A small circle of followers began to grow around him, eagerly taking their training in the ways of Islam and *tariqah* at his hands.

From this humble beginning, the circle has grown to include thousands of *murids* or disciples in various countries of the world, among whom are to be found many eminent individuals, both religious and secular. Shaykh Nazim is a luminous, tremendously impressive spiritual personality, radiating love, compassion and goodness. He is regarded by many of his *murids* as the *qutub* or chief saint of this time.

The shaykh teaches through a subtle interweaving of personal example and talks ("Associations" or *sohbets*), invariably delivered extempore according to the inspirations that are given to him. He does not lecture, but rather pours out from his heart into the hearts of his listeners such knowledge and wisdoms as may change their innermost being and bring them toward their Lord as His humble, willing, loving servants.

Shaykh Nazim's language and style are unique, so eloquent, moving and flavorful that not only do his teachings seem inspired but also his extraordinary use of words. His *sohbets* represent the teachings of a twentieth century Sufi master, firmly grounded in Islamic orthodoxy, speaking to the hearts of the seekers of God of any faith tradition from his own great, wide heart, in a tremendous outpouring of truth, wisdom and divine knowledge which is surely unparalleled in the English language, guiding the seeker toward the Divine Presence.

The sum total of Shaykh Nazim's message is that of hope, love, mercy and reassurance. In a troubled and uncertain world in which old, time-honored values have given place to new ones of confused origins and unclear prospects, in which a feeling heart and thinking mind is constantly troubled by a sense of things being terribly disordered and out of control, in which the future seems forebodingly dark and uncertain for humanity, he proclaims God's love and care for His servants, and invites them to give their hearts to Him.

Shaykh Nazim holds out to seekers the assurance that even their smallest steps toward their Lord will not go unnoticed and unresponded to. Rather than threatening sinners with the prospect of eternal Hell, he offers hope of salvation from the Most Merciful Lord, and heart-warming encouragement and incentive for inner change and growth. As one who has traversed every step of the seeker's path and reached its pinnacle, he offers both spiritual and practical guidelines for attaining the highest spiritual goals.

Volumes One through Five in this series constist of Shaykh Nazim's talks from the Ramadans of 1984 through 1988, while Volume Six consists of a number of talks given on other occasions in various years. Each of these talks is entirely extempore, as Shaykh Nazim never prepares his words but invariably speaks according to inspirations coming to his heart.

In keeping with the shaykh's methodology—the methodology of the prophets, particularly of the Last Prophet, Muhammad, peace be upon him and upon them all, and of the Qur'an itself—of reinforcing vital lessons by repetition and reiteration, the same themes and anecdotes recur again and again. The talks seem to come in unannounced clusters, centering around a primary theme, which develops and evolves according to the spiritual state of the listeners. Thus, Shaykh Nazim may cite the same verse or *hadith*, or tell the same tale on different occasions, each time reinforcing a slightly different aspect of the eternal message of love and light that is Islam.

The shaykh's talks are interspersed with words and phrases from Arabic and other Islamic languages. These are translated either in the text itself, in footnotes the first time they occur, or, for general and recurrent terms, in the Glossary at the end of this volume. Qur'anic verses quoted in the text have been referenced for easy access.

Every attempt has been made to retain the shaykh's original language with minimal editing. However, since these talks were transcribed from audio tapes recorded on amateur equipment by listeners for their own personal use (or, in the case of Book Five, by the hand of a *murid* extremely familiar with the shaykh's language and ideas), some inadvertent errors may have found their way into the text. For these, we ask Allah's forgiveness and your kind indulgence. May He fill your heart with light and love as you read and reflect upon these inspired words, and guide you safely to His exalted Divine Presence.

publisher's note

Shaykh Nazim is fluent in Arabic, Turkish and Greek, and semi-fluent in Engish. Over three decades, his lectures have been transated into twenty or more languages, and to date have reached the furthest corners of the globe. We sincerely hope the reader will appreciate the author's unique language style, which has been painstakingly preserved in this work.

As some of the terms in this book may be foreign, to assist the reader we have provded transliterations, as well as a detailed glossary.

notes

The following symbols are universally recognized and have been respectfully included in this work:

The symbol ﷺ stands for *"Salla-Lahu 'alayhi wa sallam,"* meaning, "Allah's peace and blessings be upon him," the Islamic invocation for Prophet Muhammad.

The symbol ﷺ stands for *"'Alayhi/'Alayha-s-salam,"* the Islamic invocation for angels, prophets other than Muhammad, and certain holy personages such as Sayyidina Khidr, the blessed Virgin Mary and the Mahdi.

The symbol ﷺ stands for *"Radi-Allahu 'anhu/anha,"* the Islamic invocation for the male/female Companions of the Prophet.

In the Name of Allah, The Beneficent and The Munificent

This, my English, is strange English. Not everyone can understand because, *subhanallah*, meanings are coming to my heart, and when running in my heart to give to you, I am using any means—from here, from there—bringing any word which may be useful.

I am like a person waiting for water to run out from the faucet. Then, when suddenly it comes, and he knows the water is going to be turned off, stop running, he may take any container—with a no-good shape, broken on one side, or anything he may find there—quickly bringing them to take that water and store it. Therefore, when meanings are coming to my heart, I am trying to explain with any word, which you may understand or not. But you must understand, because we have a saying, "Listeners must be more wise than speakers." Therefore, when inspiration comes, we must explain.

They are living words, not plastic—bananas, plastic; apples, plastic, and grapes. Even if the shapes are not much, they are living, real. When you are going to arrange them in measures, good system, when you are going to be engaged by outside forms, you are losing meanings. ▲

1: Taking Away the Veil Between Ourselves and Our Lord

By the name of Allah, All-Mighty, All-Merciful, Most Beneficent and Most Munificent.

We are asking from our Lord endless Mercy Oceans for the occasion of Holy Ramadan. This holy month is for the whole universe, for all the children of Adam.

Allah Almighty is *ar-Rahman,*[1] and He has endless Mercy Oceans. He has ninety-nine Beautiful Names, and each holy Name has a Mercy Ocean and each Mercy Ocean is endless. *Ar-Rahman* is one of the ninety-nine Beautiful Names, and its Mercy Oceans in the universe are making everything to appear from endless Power Oceans.

Everyone, every creature, takes its share from those Mercy Oceans that belong to the holy Name of *ar-Rahman.* Everything in existence *must* take a share from that Mercy Ocean; believers and unbelievers, they take their shares from that holy Name. During this entire month, the holy month of Ramadan, those Mercy Oceans are raining on all the people living on this earth. And we are asking, through those Mercy Oceans, forgiveness and endless favors from Allah Almighty.

Each prophet brought a message from the Lord, Allah Almighty, and the Last Prophet, beloved Muhammad ﷺ, brought the last Message, and it is the perfect one. He brought that Message over twenty-three years. The whole Qur'an, the Holy Qur'an, the Glorious Qur'an, guides people to the unity of Allah Almighty. All the prophets came just to proclaim that there

---

[1]The Most Merciful, Beneficent and Compassionate.

is no God but Almighty Allah and that absolute existence is for Allah Almighty only.

Now, we are here, we are in existence. One hundred years ago none of these people was in existence, and perhaps one hundred years from now none of us will be in existence. Therefore, our existence in this world has been given to ourselves by Someone and then it is going to be taken from us, so that no one can claim that we are something having existence, absolute existence. That is only for One, whose existence *must be*. That One causes everything to be in existence, and we have been called into existence to proclaim the unity of Allah Almighty.

Allah Almighty gave us, the children of Adam, ego, *nafs*, so that we have a special station, a special place, among all creatures. More than any other creature we have been honored. If we hadn't been given egos, we would be like angels, but Allah Almighty made the children of Adam to be deputies for Him on the earth and in the universe. All of us, we are candidates to be deputies, *khalifahs*, of Allah Almighty here and Hereafter.

Then, everyone has that opportunity or chance to be a real deputy of Allah Almighty, and each prophet came just to teach and to guide and to show people how they can reach that position of being real deputies. As many as there are children of Adam in existence, in the Divine Presence we have thrones, and each one's name is written on one of them. If we can do our best during this life, we have a way to reach that throne and sit on it in the Divine Presence. Therefore, we must have some method, some teaching, so that we may be able to reach that throne and sit on it.

We have been invited by Allah Almighty to come and sit on that seat in His Divine Presence. It is the top point of honor that can be given by Allah Almighty to His creatures, and it is for *us*. We are very fortunate ones among all creatures. Even the angels, they were asking for that honor to be for themselves,[2] but Allah Almighty just appointed that honor for the chil-

---

[2] Referring to the words of the angels in Paradise when they asked their Lord, "Will You place on it [the earth] one who causes corruption therein and sheds blood, while we proclaim Your praise and sanctify You?" (2:30)

3

dren of Adam. They may be black ones, may be white ones, may be yellow ones, may be red ones; no worry. Pakistanis, also, they are candidates for that; African people, also, not only European people, no; Asian people, also. Each one whose name is written among the children of Adam, they are candidates, they have seats in the Divine Presence.

Allah Almighty does not look at our shapes, our forms. He looks at our hearts. And He put there in our hearts a very precious thing, and it has been protected by divine protection; no one may be able to take that precious thing from our hearts. Satan is running after it, but even if there were millions of satans and their powers all came together, it would be impossible to take away that precious point from the hearts of the children of Adam, whether they are English or French or Russian or unbelievers.

Allah Almighty gave that honor to everyone, not only to Muslims or to believers, but *all* people have that honor from Allah Almighty. And it is in a safe place, and the Guardian of that point in the hearts of the sons of Adam is Almighty Allah. No one can touch that; it remains there. Divine lights burn anyone who may put his hand there; it is impossible. And Allah Almighty is calling us to His Divine Presence, to take our seats, inviting us to His divine feast in His Divine Presence.

Now we are living in this life and we do not know about ourselves yet. You have been created for the love of Allah Almighty! Your heart has been put inside you to be the place at which Allah Almighty looks, and He put from His love into the hearts of the children of Adam and your honor comes from that. He loved and He created, and His divine love is in every heart of the children of Adam.

We do not know about ourselves. We know only who we are, as, "I am Muhammad Knight, a Scottish person, a teacher"—name, surname, father's name, mother's name, motherland and nothing else. And your knowing about yourself is the entrance to divine knowledge about your Lord. When you know about yourself, that is an opening to the Lord's knowledge.

People now are asking a question but it is not a right one. They are beginning to ask about the Creator, about Allah Almighty, who He is, how

He is, while leaving themselves. You must ask about yourself, "Who am I? What is my position in the universe? What is the meaning of being from mankind? Who are they?" You must begin from yourself and *then* you may ask who is the Creator, how He is, who He is. We are asking questions in the opposite way, and anyone who leaves himself and asks about the Creator, he is never going to reach an understanding of the Lord, Allah Almighty.

We must understand and we must know about ourselves first. And all knowledge and perfect information about ourselves was brought by the Last Prophet, the Seal of the Prophets, peace be upon him and upon them, in the Holy Qur'an. And we are in need of an opening. Without an opening, you can't enter it.

Therefore, the Holy Qur'an has an opening; the first *surah* is the *Surah* of Opening. That *surah* gives us details about everything, about ourselves and about the Lord, Allah Almighty, and the relationship between ourselves and our Lord. And we must return to that Opening.

It is impossible for a servant to reach that point without understanding about his ego. He must understand about his ego because ego becomes a hindrance, preventing you from reaching your reality in existence. Always that ego is coming and covering it; always ego is preventing a person and not letting him reach real knowledge about himself. Therefore, we have been ordered to take away that huge veil and hindrance. If you aren't able to take it away, you won't be able to reach the reality of the real knowledge about yourself that makes a way for you to reach the Divine Presence and divine knowledge.

The first man and first prophet, Adam ﷺ, was with his Lord, Allah Almighty; originally, he was in Paradise, he was with his Lord, seeing and hearing. But when his ego made a trap for him, then a huge barrier, a huge veil, came between his Lord and himself, making him to come down. And that huge veil comes among his children; as long as they are living on earth, that veil is between themselves and their Lord. And Adam ﷺ was told that if you can take it away, the barrier of your ego, quickly you may be with your Lord, as before.[3]

Our Lord is with us but we do not feel that. We think that the Lord is on His Throne, too far away, or that our Lord will be with us on the Last Day. No one thinks or feels that our Lord is with ourselves and that without our Lord we can't be in existence for even a minute or a second, or less than a second. You can't be in existence if your Lord is not with you. All things are standing in existence by their Lord; if He was not there, nothing would be in existence. But we are heedless. We are not considering or thinking that Allah Almighty is with ourselves, we are making Him far away.

That is ego, coming and making a huge veil. You can't see it, you can't think about it. Therefore, from the beginning, from the time of Adam, we have been ordered to take away that veil and to be with our Lord, Allah Almighty. We have been ordered to cut away that veil, and all worshipping and all shar'iats[4] are for taking away our ego and its veils.

The most effective action for taking away that veil is fasting. Therefore Allah Almighty ordered every nation, through every prophet, to fast, and we are fasting for that purpose: to take away our ego's veil and to be with our Lord.

When Allah Almighty spoke to Moses ﷺ on Sinai, between Moses and his Lord there were 70,000 veils. And Allah Almighty ordered the nation of Muhammad ﷺ to fast, and He says that when the time of breaking fast comes, I leave only one veil between Myself and My fasting servant. If we could cut that veil, we would be with our Lord, Allah Almighty; we would be in Unity Oceans, and you can't come back from that Ocean. Therefore Allah Almighty is keeping that one veil between you and Himself until we finish our period in this life. Otherwise, anyone who reaches the time of breaking fast would be taken away and disappear; he would be with his Lord at break-fast in the Divine Presence.

---

[3]Referring to, "And if, as is sure, there comes to you guidance from Me, then whoever follows My guidance, no fear shall come upon them, nor shall they grieve." (20:123 and 2:38)

[4]Sacred laws revealed by God through His prophets.

We are thanking our Lord that He gave us such a powerful means for coming closer to His Divine Presence, and we hope that one day, when our lives are ended, we will be in His Divine Presence and that He will grant us to be in His Divine Presence forever. And therefore we must try to take away that veil between ourselves and our Lord, Allah Almighty. ▲

2: the importance of believing in and following the holy prophet

O our Lord, we are nothing, or trying to be nothing. You are in existence, and for the sake of Your Holy Prophet, beloved Muhammad 🌸, we are in existence. All glory and praise and thanks to You, O our Lord. Grant us those things that we are in need of. We are intending to be obedient servants and we are asking Your divine help.

We are sitting here to learn how we can be obedient servants. That is important for our lives, because we have been invited to the Divine Presence. The Last Day will come and everyone must die, and then Allah Almighty will bring them to life in His Divine Presence. Everyone must believe that there is a Gathering Day and that, as he came to this life and knew nothing, the One who sent him to this life will also bring him to the next life in His Divine Presence.

We are intending to be obedient servants to our Lord, Allah Almighty. The way that reaches that station of being obedient servants to our Lord passes through believing in His beloved Muhammad 🌸, and our faith also lies in believing in beloved Muhammad 🌸. And for everyone, belief in beloved Muhammad 🌸 must be through knowing him and recognizing him and loving him.

Allah Almighty sent each prophet among his own people, and He made each one to be the most noble person among his nation. Each prophet was a perfect one in his physical body and a perfect one in his mind. They were perfect-looking, also, because Allah Almighty made them in perfection outwardly and inwardly, since those people who are calling to Allah Almighty must be in perfection. It is not divine wisdom to send to people a person in whom, if they look at him, they see anything that makes them dislike him. Therefore, they were perfect outwardly and in their souls;

their appearance and their physical bodies were perfect, and their characteristics were also perfect.

And the Last Prophet, also, our prophet, Sayyidina Muhammad ﷺ, was in perfection outwardly; if anyone looked at him, he was carried away. And Allah Almighty also gave him such characteristics that Muhammad ﷺ was unique among all prophets, among all creatures. No one can reach our prophet's perfection in his physical body or in his characteristics.

Allah Almighty praises him for having the best characteristics.[5] Allah gave to him from His attributes, and our prophet is the most perfect one among prophets, among all people, with every perfection that a person can have. Therefore, knowledge about the Holy Prophet ﷺ must be learned by everyone. The more we can learn about beloved Muhammad ﷺ, the more our hearts will run toward him with love.

Firstly, Allah Almighty gave him the most beautiful names. Muhammad ﷺ means "the Praised One"; here and Hereafter, on earth and in the Heavens, he has been praised. And then Allah Almighty gave him the best of every good characteristic. All prophets have the characteristic of being truthful; they never told lies. And our prophet, up to time when prophethood came to him, was known as the truest one among his tribe, among his nation, and he was called *"Muhammad al-Amin,"*[6] the one who was, throughout his life, the truest one.

He was the prophet before creation appeared; no creation had yet appeared when his name was written as prophet in the Divine Presence. *"La ilaha illa-Llah, Muhammadu Rasul-Allah,* There is no God but Allah and Muhammad is His messenger," was written on the Divine Throne; the first writing was *"La ilaha illa-Llah, Muhammadu Rasul-Allah."* That writing of *"La ilaha illa-Llah"* is never found without *"Muhammadu Rasul-Allah,"* ﷺ. No one knows at which time *"La ilaha illa-Llah"* was written; in pre-eternity it was written, although no one can known when, and after it was written *"Muhammadu Rasul-Allah"* ﷺ.

---

[5] "And you (Muhammad) stand on an exalted standard of character." (64:4)
[6] Muhammad, the Trustworthy.

He was the first among creatures, the first among prophets, and his nation, also, was created first, but Allah Almighty sent him after all the other prophets, as when there is an invitation and the king is invited to that feast. The king does not come first but comes last—yes? Therefore, the Seal of the Prophets was the first among creation but he was the last of the prophets to come to this world.

And when he came, for forty years he never said or proclaimed anything about his prophethood. Then, when he reached forty years, Allah Almighty sent the angel Gabriel and ordered Muhammad ﷺ to proclaim that he was a prophet, the Last Prophet, the prophet for everyone on earth, here and Hereafter.

And people around him were surprised. They said, "How can he say this? He never told a lie throughout his life but now he is saying something that we can't accept. We are worshiping idols; so many idols we are praying to, and now he is saying that all your idols are *batil*, false, that you must leave them and you must worship the Lord of the Heavens, the Lord of the worlds, the Lord of the children of Adam." They were so surprised, saying, "How is that one calling us to something that we have never even heard about, while he has never told a lie? What shall we do?"

But he was truthful, the truest one who ever lived on earth. And his invitation was correct because he was inviting all people to the Divine Presence and he came to bring people to his way, and whoever comes on his way is going to be beloved by his Lord, Almighty Allah. Therefore, he was calling to a way. The one who can be on it can be a saint, a *wali*, a beloved one to his Lord, Allah Almighty.

And his Message is continuing up to today; his invitation is continuing throughout East and West. He is calling people to their Lord, to Allah Almighty. He is not calling people to worship himself or to be servants to him, but he is calling people and saying, "O people, I am a servant of your Lord. Your Lord is my Lord. All of you, you must come and must be obedient servants and worshippers of your Lord. He gave to me from His divine love and I represent divine love. Nothing is more precious in the Divine Presence than divine love, and I have come to give you what my

Lord gave to me from His divine love. I am coming, O people, O my Lord's servants, and asking to make you sharers in that love. I am bringing love to humanity. My Lord gave it to me. Therefore, I am *beloved* Muhammad," he says, "and I have brought you divine love. Come and take! I am giving."

Anything better than this? Who can consider anything to be more precious or more valuable than this? And in the Divine Presence there are endless Love Oceans. That love makes you 'high'! Yes, that is also the meaning of making you high; 'high' is also to live our life with love, in divine love.

Therefore, the Last Prophet, the Seal of the Prophets, just brought to the world divine love. We can't carry it by ourselves. The love of the Lord, Allah Almighty, comes to the Prophet's heart, and then, through the Prophet's heart it goes through *awliya's* hearts, and *awliya's* hearts are sources of divine love. Anyone who finds our Lord's *awliya* and goes to their hearts, he takes his share of divine love.

You must know about the Last Prophet. We just gave a very short description of him, but it may be enough for anyone to know about beloved Muhammad ﷺ. When you think about his name, it is enough for you to know him and to love him, also. Allah Almighty loves him and gives to him, and he is calling us to his way.

And Allah Almighty gave him five hundred commands. Anyone may be able to practice all of them or some of them, and the divine wisdom in giving those five hundred commands is that for each one that we are practicing, we are taking more share from divine Love Oceans.

All of them are acts of worship or of charity. Worshipping is for your Lord and charity is for His servants and the creatures of your Lord, Allah Almighty, and both of them make Him pleased with you. Every worship makes your Lord pleased with you, and every charity that you do for His creatures and for His servants also makes Him pleased with you. And if Allah Almighty is pleased with you, then He grants to you more love from His divine Love Oceans. That is the message of the Last Prophet; that is the way of beloved Muhammad ﷺ, showing us how to reach to that, so that we may have more share of Love Oceans, divine Love Oceans.

Then, Allah Almighty, through His Prophet, also prohibits certain actions, the actions of devils. Evils are the actions of devils, and He prevents and prohibits His servants from those, saying, "Don't do this, don't do that." And as long as you are saying, "O our Lord, for Your sake I am leaving this bad action or this bad characteristic of my ego," then everything that you are leaving for the sake of the Lord, Allah Almighty, is making Him pleased with you, and you will come spiritually closer to Allah Almighty and He will give you more love, more share of divine Love Oceans.
▲

3: love of allah

By the name of Allah, All-Mighty, All-Merciful, Most Beneficent and Most Munificent, the Lord of Abraham, the Lord of Moses, the Lord of Jesus Christ, the Lord of beloved Muhammad, peace be upon him and upon them.

We are asking Allah Almighty's blessings during this holy month, and asking also that His blessings continue forever for ourselves and for each one of the children of Adam, and that He keeps us from misguidance and misguided people, because man, during this life, may be guided or may be misguided. Those who are misguided, their ways are going to Hells here and Hereafter, and the ones who have been guided, their way is going to Paradise here and Hereafter. Therefore, we are in need of praying to our Lord and asking Him for guidance in our lives, and, as His servants ask, He gives guidance.

That is an important thing for our lives, to ask for guidance from our Lord, Allah Almighty. People are between *haqq* and *batil*, truth and falsehood, and everyone must learn and must know what is truth and falsehood. We are in need to follow truth throughout our lives because it gives us honor and peace here and Hereafter, while falsehood grows from misguidance and makes troubles, giving sufferings to people here and Hereafter.

Our Grandshaykh, may Allah bless him, was saying, "When a person accepts truth, when he proclaims truth first by his tongue, then that truth must come to his heart." First he proclaims it with his tongue and believes it in his heart, confirming or acknowledging it.

What is going to happen when truth is in someone's heart? What is the sign that a person has truth and that he has accepted truth in his heart? There must be a sign.

Allah Almighty says in His Glorious Qur'an, *"Wa qul: Ja'a al-haqq wa zahaq al-batil*—when truth comes, falsehood goes away; truth defeats falsehood."[7] Therefore, when we proclaim truth with our tongues, it prevents our tongues from uttering any falsehood. Then, more than that, when our hearts accept truth and truth is in our hearts, it also takes away every falsehood from our hearts.

The first thing, when truth comes into our hearts, is that it takes away every bad thought and bad intention and bad characteristic. In our books that have come through traditions from every prophet up to the Seal of the Prophets, beloved Muhammad 器, it is stated that there are so many bad characteristics in our hearts, in number sixty false and bad characteristics within our hearts. When truth comes, it takes those away, defeating them.

The first and most dangerous falsehood is *kufr*, to deny the existence of the Lord, Almighty Allah. When truth comes, a person must believe in the existence of the Lord, Almighty Allah; he must say that there is a Creator who created all the worlds, who created the universe, who created the Heavens, who created Paradise and Hells. Truth makes him proclaim and believe that there is one Lord, creating, giving life, and taking life away. And that is the first and most important thing when truth enters into our hearts: to proclaim the existence of the Lord, Almighty Allah.

Then, we proclaim that the Lord, Almighty Allah, has eternal existence from pre-eternity up to post-eternity, and we proclaim the truth that there is an eternal life for the children of Adam—for believers and for unbelievers, also, because those who do not believe in eternal life are not going to die and finish, no. They also have eternal life, and truth in our hearts makes us believe in that eternal life.

No need to believe in *this* life because we are living in it, but, when we are believers, we believe in unseen things, and the way to our Lord passes through unseen territories. We believe in the life unseen. If you want to see, you must first believe in the Unseen; then you may see it, you may

---

[7](17:81)

reach that point. Therefore, we believe in unseen worlds and heavens, and we believe in the eternal life.

That is the result of accepting truth, taking away, one after the other, the bad characteristics from our hearts. When truth comes, falsehood must go away. Every bad characteristic belongs to falsehood, and if real truth comes and enters into your heart, it must take that away. And one of the biggest falsehoods and worst characteristics of the children of Adam is that they like this life. The love of *dunya*, the love of this life—that is the biggest sin, which is the source of evils.

As long as people love this *dunya*, this life, troubles will never go away. Each day they will fall down more, sinking into sufferings. Therefore, if truth comes to your heart, it takes away the love of *dunya* and changes that love into the love of your Lord, the love of Allah Almighty. That is the sign that you love your Lord, defeating in your heart the love of this world, the love of this life, because if we give our love to a temporary thing and it goes away, our love finishes. But that love is something that has been given to us to put in a suitable place.

Once the angel Gabriel ﷺ came to Prophet Muhammad ﷺ and said to him, "O Muhammad, you may put your love with anyone whom you select. As you like, you may put your love with that thing. But you must know that everything that you love in this world is going to leave you."

If you put your love with your family, with your wife, with your children, with your business, with your car, with your castle, with your ranks—with anything or anyone you may put your love with, you must know that it will go away and leave you, and your love will go with it and finish, so that it is falsehood to put our love there because Allah Almighty gives us that love and it is divine.

You must be very careful where you put that precious thing, whether losing it or protecting it. If you give your love during your life to anyone—to your wife or your children or your castle or your business—then it is lost, finished, because when you leave this life, that love will not be with you. Those people or those things will stay here and you will go without love; your love will stay behind.

That is falsehood. But when truth comes to your heart, truth says to you, "Don't give your love except to the eternal existence of your Lord, Allah Almighty. Give Him your love because that love comes from Him. Give it back to Him, also." When you are here, that love is with you; if you go, it goes with you. You are with your Lord here and when you go from this life, He does not leave you; He is with you forever. In the eternal life, also, He is with you, and you are not going to lose your love. You will gain it because you have put it with the correct and suitable One.

Therefore, truth, when it comes to the heart of a person—he may be a Christian, he may be Jewish, he may be Buddhist, he may be Muslim; no difference—that love of the Lord with truth must be in that person's heart. Otherwise he is a liar. A real Muslim, a real Christian, a real Jew, a real Buddhist, a real Zoroastrian, must have truth with himself. If falsehood is in his heart, he will run to this life's enjoyments and he will represent falsehood. The one who represents truth, his heart must be with his Lord; he must give his love only to his Lord, Almighty Allah.

Therefore, we are asking for that truth. Don't cheat yourself and don't cheat others. Everyone must look into his heart, at who is there. His love is with whom—with very temporary things or with the eternal Lord, Allah Almighty?

We must think about it, because our breaths are limited. Each day, 24,000 breaths are finishing, and we have a limited number, millions or billions. Their number is written, and every moment, every second, we are taking and finishing them. Then, before our breaths finish, we must look after ourselves, at where we are putting our love. We still have an opportunity to change that love from temporary things to the eternal and permanent existence. That is important.

Every prophet just came to make it firm for everyone, so that they may give their love only to their Lord. "O people, your Lord gave you that love and He is asking it back from you to Himself." That is important.

We are not playing. We have not come into this life to play with families, with wives, with children—no. There are some places in our bodies which belong to children, to wives, to animals, to farms, to flowers, but love is for Allah Almighty only. And the main sign comes: when truth enters into your heart, when that love goes to Allah, it takes falsehood away. And that is falsehood, to put your love with temporary things; *that is falsehood.* You must change it, you must give your love to the eternal existence of Allah Almighty, the Lord. We must try to do it.

Titles are not important: Muslim, Christian, Jewish, to be a shaykh, to be a priest, to be a rabbi, to put a big thing on your head—no. Important is this: to whom you are giving that love. The One who gave you that love, you must give it to Him. No one else is suitable for that love; only your Lord, and He will ask on the Day of Resurrection, "What did you bring, O My servant? What did you bring to Me?"

Fasting, praying, giving charities, going on pilgrimage—all of them are for what? *For the sake of that love; you are giving your love to your Lord.* Present Him with fasting, with worshipping; every kind of worshipping makes you present your love to His Divine Presence. Yes; the real aim of every kind of worshipping and charity is to say, "O my Lord, I am presenting to You my love through this worship. It is not suitable for You, our worshipping. We can only give You our love." And He is asking that love from His servants.

If everyone gathered and gave their love to their Lord, this life would be a paradise. But we are *not* giving our love to our Lord; we are only giving something, some nonsensical things, and we are living in hell. Our lives are full of sadness, of fear, of hopeless things, of troubles and sufferings. That is the reason, because falsehood is in our hearts; truth has not yet come and entered into your heart to defeat falsehood from your heart. Yes, everyone is carrying his responsibility.

May falsehood be taken away from your heart and truth come and enter into your heart, and may Allah Almighty make for you a private situation in a private world. You may be with people, you may walk with them in this life, but you will see some other ones. You will live in another London city, not *this* London. There is another London, also; there is not only one London for the Lord, Almighty Allah. He is the Creator, and when He orders there to be in existence one billion Londons for His sincere servants, they are ready. Yes; that is the truth, and when truth comes, falsehood goes away.

The one who has truth in his heart may live in another London with other ones, with some people whose faces are like sunshine. Their roads, their streets are clean; no sound harms your senses; no one looks at another with wildness. Silver domes, golden towers. Yes, that is the *barakah* of be-ing with truth. "When truth comes, falsehood goes away,"[8] Allah Almighty says.

Therefore we are asking forgiveness for everything, and we are asking divine help for taking away falsehood from our hearts and putting that truth into our hearts, truth going through our bodies, through our minds and around ourselves. May Allah give it to you.

When I am saying something, I have been authorized to give that good tidings to you through my Grandshaykh. *You* must see it, also. Therefore, when I am saying that there are other Londons, you may see them. When truth comes clearly into your heart, it is so easy. I may take you to that London. *Wa min Allah at-tawfiq.*[9] ▲

---

[8](17:8)
[9]And success is from Allah.

4: keeping our hearts with allah almighty

By the name of Allah, All-Mighty, All-Merciful, Most Beneficent and Most Munificent. He knows what we are in need of and He gives what we are in need of. Believers, they are in need of divine support throughout their lives, and the one who has strong faith and belief, he receives more support. And also, the more we know we are weak and in need, Allah Almighty gives us more support.

Our Grandshaykh was always speaking about the good attribute which is more lovely to Allah Almighty than anything else. Allah Almighty likes His servant to ask from Him and to say, "O my Lord, I am Your weakest and most needy one." This attribute of servants is most lovely to our Lord, Allah Almighty, and we are saying, "O our Lord, we are the weakest ones and the most in need of Your divine support." And Allah Almighty gives that support, and if we are sincere, He gives to us also from His endless favors.

We are in a holy month, and that holy month is teaching us. Fasting teaches servants that they are in need of their Lord at all times. And when a person fasts and thinks about his Lord, Allah Almighty looks at what is in His servant's heart, at who is there, because Allah Almighty created man and He made one part of our bodies for Himself only. He never accepts to have a partner for Himself, and the most precious part of your body is *that* part. Your heart is that precious one, and it belongs to the Lord, Almighty Allah.

And He looks there; each day Allah Almighty looks at our hearts. Why does He look? He looks to see what His servant is doing with that precious part. Allah Almighty says, "O My servant, My face is toward your face, but *your* face is toward what? O My servant, put your face in front of My Divine Face." But your face is mostly *not* in front of His Divine Face, and we are asking forgiveness.

All prophets and all *shari'ats* came to teach people that they must put their faces in front of their Lord's Divine Face. People are running after finding peace and happiness and satisfaction through this world, but it is impossible. If you are looking and your face is not toward your Lord's Divine Face, no one can find peace and satisfaction and happiness in his heart. And each day Allah Almighty is looking and trying His servants, to see whether His servant is with Him or is with someone else.

Once there was a grandshaykh, and one day he went up to the *mimbar*[10] for the *Jumu'a khutbah*, addressing a huge crowd of people; so many scholars, they were listening to him, also. And he was saying, "O people, look at me and listen! Judgment Day is approaching, and everyone must be present on that Day, the Last Day, the judgment day for everyone. And the Judge, He is your Lord, Allah Almighty.

"Don't be afraid! He is only going to call you one by one; He can do anything! He will make judgment on everyone one by one and at the same time He will make judgment for everyone, and everyone will think that Allah Almighty, his Lord, is judging him only, while He is really going to give judgment for everyone who is in that place.

"He will call you and ask you only one question, nothing else." And they were listening carefully. "If you can give a correct answer, it will be all right; no need to ask a second question. If not, it will be difficult for you. Your Lord will ask everyone, will ask you, 'O my servant, I was with you during your life. You—with whom were you?'"

That is the question, only one question: "O *My servant, with whom were you?*" That is the question. If you can say, "O my Lord, I was with *You*," then every question will have been given its answer and your Lord will be

---

[10]The elevated pulpit from which the Friday (*Jumu'a*) sermon (*khutba*) is delivered.

happy with you, pleased with you; you will have made Him pleased with you. But if not, too much trouble is waiting for you.

Therefore, each prophet just came to teach us how we should be with our Lord at all times and how we must try to be with Him throughout our lives. Therefore, Allah Almighty made every action of mankind to be governed by a rule.

Each moment and each action has a value, and you must consider the value of your actions and you must think about that action. When you are going to act, you must know that Someone is looking at you and that that Someone is your Lord. His Face, His Divine Face, is toward your heart, and His Divine Face and Its gaze is on you.

When you keep that *adab*, good manners, then your Lord, Allah Almighty, is going to be with you, at every time. With His endless favors He will support you for everything; as long as you consider your Lord, more support will come to you. And our Grandshaykh was always speaking about real faith, acceptable faith—how it must be so that Allah Almighty accepts that faith, and which kind of faith supports its owner, divine support always protecting him.

We must consider always in our hearts that Allah Almighty, by day or night throughout out whole life, is looking at us. His divine gaze is never taken away from anyone. If you consider that my shaykh is looking at me everywhere, you will be careful about every action that you are going to do. Then what about Allah Almighty, never leaving you even for the smallest unit of time, looking at you? *That* gives us real faith in Allah Almighty.

If Allah Almighty gives to us from His favors, sometimes we forget our Lord because we are occupied with the enjoyment of favors during this life. But Allah Almighty gives His servants mostly troubles.

When Allah created man, Adam, He had not yet blown into him from His divine Spirit, so that only Adam's body was lying, without a soul. Then Allah Almighty ordered a rain to fall on him. It rained for forty years only sadness; sadness, sorrow and suffering rained on his body. Then it stopped, and for one year it rained a rain of enjoyment and happiness.

Therefore, in forty years, only one year of happiness and enjoyment comes during our lives. What is the divine wisdom in that? There are so many wisdoms for that rain on Adam, and on his children, also, it is the same.

If a person speaks to his Lord, calling Him, *"Ya Karim!"*[11] Allah Almighty calls to His servant and says, "O My servant, you are still in that world, you are in prison. Then how are you saying *Ya Karim*? What do you know about My *karam*, My favors? This world, this life, is a prison for everyone, for believers and unbelievers. You must be patient. When you get to Paradise, Paradise is the place of My favors. This world, this life, is not yet the place of My favors!"

Troubles and sufferings and sorrows always cover this life, O people, and you can only breathe through your beliefs. Those who believe, they may take themselves out of that sorrow and sadness, but the ones who haven't any beliefs or faith, they are always in darkness, in sadness, in sorrow. And the divine wisdom of Allah Almighty's making too many sufferings and sorrows for man here is because when we are in sadness, in troubles and suffering, we ask for someone to help us. *"Ya Aman, ya Rabbi!"*[12] we must say, we must call to Him.

When we are rich, we think that we are not in need of anyone and we do not call to Him, but when we are in trouble, then we remember that One who can help us in any condition, in any situation. Therefore, throughout our whole life, suffering powers our lives. Allah Almighty likes His servants to call Him and to ask from Him. When you call, "O my God!" He says, "O My servant!" and without your heart burning, that addressing to Allah does not come. If that calling to Allah comes from your heart, He accepts it; if it only comes from your lips, it does not reach there as it does when it comes from your heart. Therefore Allah Almighty makes sorrows and sufferings for His servants so that they may remember Him and His blessings and favors.

---

[11]"O Most Beneficent, Generous, Gracious One!"
[12]"O Trustworthy One, O my Lord!"

And Allah Almighty is always trying His servants; everyone is going to be tried. Trying makes our faith stronger. If He does not try you, you will stay on the same level, and therefore Allah Almighty tries His servants and gives them more power through their beliefs and faith. Therefore, everything that comes upon people is a trial from Allah Almighty. And the Prophet ﷺ says, "If two days of your life are equal, the same, it is a loss. Today must be more than yesterday and tomorrow must be more than this day."

What does it mean? It does not mean that if you pray forty *rak'ats*[13] today, you are going to do forty-one tomorrow and after tomorrow forty-two—no. But as we grow in our mother's womb and come to this life, and grow day by day from a one-day-old baby, a two-day-old baby, then one week, one month, one year, we grow up to forty years. Forty years, it is a perfection for our physical body and for our mind. Then, from forty, our physical body begins to go down, becoming weaker, but our spiritual power must go on to perfection. Day by day our faith must reach to a point that, when you reach that level, there should be a new world in your view.

Now all of us, we are going through a black tunnel. But we must continue on our steps. Then we will reach that horizon and we will see another world that is now unseen to ourselves. If you reach that point before leaving this life, you are fortunate. You will have reached the real position of being deputy of your Lord, Almighty Allah.

That is the meaning of that *hadith*, that saying of the Prophet ﷺ, that day by day we must approach that horizon. If you stay on the same step, then you are losing; each day you must put your foot on the next step. Before death comes, you must finish your steps and you must be at that horizon, looking at unseen worlds, looking at the Heavens, looking at your heavenly station in the Divine Presence. Those are fortunate people, *rijal-Allah*.[14]

---

[13]Cycles of *salat*, the Islamic prayer.
[14]People of Allah.

Therefore, Allah Almighty is trying His servants every day. And believers, they know that there is trying by Allah Almighty and they are preparing themselves to carry it. It may be by anything, any kind of a trial. And mostly Allah Almighty tries His servants by each other, and He likes you to carry each other without getting angry. Anger is wildness and Allah Almighty never likes it. And every day, from morning time up to sleeping time, you must be awake, seeing from where a trial is coming to you, so that you may be ready to keep that. If you keep it—one step more, one step more—your faith gets to be stronger.

This holy month is teaching us, also, to bear, to be patient, and to be able to carry everything that is difficult for our ego. Every difficult thing makes our faith stronger, and as much as our faith gets stronger, we are coming closer to our Lord and to His Divine Presence. ▲

5: the importance of believing in allah's existence

Allah Almighty honored us, the children of Adam 🕊, making us candidates to be the deputies of our Lord in this world, in this universe. And honor for the children of Adam is to believe in their Lord, that He is in existence and that there is no God in existence but Allah Almighty.

From the first prophet up to the last one, Allah Almighty informed and proclaimed His existence and His unity to His servants. Allah proclaimed His existence and unity through the first prophet, and He also announced it through His Last Prophet, the Seal of the Prophets, beloved Muhammad 🕊. And whoever accepts that, he has been honored by the Lord, Almighty Allah.

As we believe in all the prophets without making any distinction among them, at the beginning, all mankind was ordered or invited to believe in all the prophets, past or to come, and particularly in beloved Muhammad, peace be upon him and upon them.[15] His name was written on the Divine Throne before creatures were created, and *'La ilaha illa-Llah, Muhammadu Rasul-Allah,* there is no God but Allah and Muhammad is His messenger,*"* is written in Arabic words everywhere in Paradise, also.

And it was proclaimed by each prophet. Each prophet called his nation to believe in the Last Prophet, beloved Muhammad 🕊, because to be-

---

[15]Referring to the verse, "And [recall, O People of the Scripture] when Allah took the covenant of the prophets, [saying], 'Whatever I give you of the scripture and wisdom, and then there comes to you a messenger confirming what is with you, you [are to] believe in him and support him." He [Allah] said, "Do you agree and accept My covenant concerning that?" They said, "We agree." He [Allah] said, "Then bear witness, and I am with you among the witnesses." (3:81)

lieve in their own prophet gave them honor, but to believe also in the Last Prophet, the Seal of the Prophets, gave them more honor and more lights. Therefore Allah Almighty invited and ordered all nations, through their prophets, to believe in their own prophets and also to believe in the Last Prophet, beloved Muhammad ﷺ; so that each prophet informed his nation about the Last Prophet through their holy books, and each holy book mentioned the Last Prophet, Muhammad ﷺ, by his name, as it is written on the pillars of the Throne, *"La ilaha illa-Llah, Muhammadu Rasul-Allah."*

Then, the last prophet before the Seal of the Prophets, Jesus Christ ﷺ, also mentioned the name of the greatest prophet and the Seal of the Prophets, Sayyidina Muhammad ﷺ, in his Gospel, *Injil,*[16] mentioning his name as "Ahmad,"[17] which they are translating as *"Parakletos"* in the original Greek Bible.[18] He was saying that Ahmad is coming just after me; he is going to be the prophet for all nations, and his nation, *ummah,* is the last of the *ummahs.*

As it is written, it was well-known also among scholars of the Christian faith. They knew from where he was going to come. It is written that the Last Prophet would come from Hijaz[19] and it is mentioned that he would come from Mecca. And also there is written every detail to make his identity exactly clear, not leaving any doubt about it, because he was the last one and must be recognized by everyone.

Since he was going to be the prophet for all the world or for all nations, he must be a well-known person among other nations—among Moses' nation and among Jesus Christ's nation and *ummah,* because he was going to come at a time when they should be ready. Therefore Allah Almighty did not leave out any sign for His beloved Muhammad ﷺ, to make His Last Prophet to be well-known, and he was indicated in holy books.

---

[16]The name given in the Qur'an to the original revelation granted to Jesus.

[17]"And remember when Jesus son of Mary said, 'O Children of Israel, indeed I am the messenger of Allah to you, confirming what came before me of the Torah and bringing good tidings of a messenger to come after me whose name is Ahmad.'" (61:6)

[18]The coming of the *Parakletos* (Paraclete) is mentioned in John 14:26; 15:26; 16:7, 13.

[19]The province of Saudi Arabia in which Mecca and Medina are located.

The Jewish people, after their Temple was destroyed, spread all over the world, everywhere. They are clever people; perhaps they are the most clever ones among all nations. And I don't think that Jewish people would leave the good places of the earth, leaving Anatolia or Syria or Iraq or Iran or Europe or Egypt or any other country, such healthy-wealthy countries, to go to the desert of Arabia; I don't think that they are such mindless people to go to live in the Arabian deserts, with fifty or sixty degrees centigrade and salty water and only palm trees growing, without any reason. Then why did they go there?

They were living in and around Yathrib and in Khaibar.[20] Why were they there, for what purpose? This *dunya*, this world, is wide, and then it was not as it is now, so crowded. No, they could go anywhere and they could live in good places, so many open spaces at that time. Then why did they choose those deserts? What was the reason?

The reason, the only reason, was that they knew that the Seal of the Prophets would come in the Arabian desert, in *that* country. It is written in the Holy Torah, in the Old Testament and the New Testament. They knew that he was going to be born *there*.

His grandfather's building was the House of the Lord.[21] Abraham ﷺ built that House, the House of the Lord, which is now there, in the middle of the desert. Nothing grew in that desert, nothing. And he said to his Lord, "O my Lord, I am leaving my descendants in a huge desert. Give them their *rizq*, provisions, and give them Your heavenly provisions, also. Send them, from Your Divine Presence, a messenger teaching them Your wisdoms and Your holy words."[22]

---

[20]Yathrib is the original name of Medina. Khaibar is a small town in northern Arabia.

[21]The Holy K'abah in Mecca.

[22]"And [mention] when Abraham said, 'My Lord, make this a secure city and provide its people with fruits—those among them that believe in Allah and the Last Day... Our Lord, and sed among them a messenger from among themselves who will recite to them Your verses and teach them the Book and wisdom and purify them. Indeed, You are the Almighty, the Wise.'" (2:126. 129)

They knew about him; it was written. And they were expecting that that prophet would come from among themselves and that they would quickly go with him, all together. But divine wisdoms made that Last Prophet from the sons of Ishmael, not from the sons of Isaac, peace be upon them both; yes. And Christians, also, were living in Najran (now it is Aden and that area) and they were also expecting that Last Prophet. It is written in traditions;[23] everything is clear in Islam.

During those years, Damascus was in the hands of the Romans, Christians. The capital of the Eastern Roman Empire was in Constantinople, and Damascus was a very famous center of Christianity at that time.

There were two priests who were always together. They were looking for the Last Prophet. Once one said to the other, "As we know through our holy books, this is the right time for the Last Prophet to appear. Let us go and search for him."

They set out to look for the Last Prophet. They began their journey from Damascus and went through deserts, reaching Yathrib. When they entered Yathrib, one of them looked at the position of the mountains and valley and trees: the valley went like this, and the mountains and their rocks were burned-looking, like black coal, and the palm trees and gardens were inside. They looked, and one of them said, "This is the place that is described in holy books. It is the place to which the Last Prophet will immigrate," because it had those special characteristics.

Then they entered Yathrib, the town, and asked for the *masjid*,[24] going there and entering. The Prophet ﷺ was there with his Companions, sitting among them.

No need for anyone to ask who *that* one was. He was like the full moon among stars. As he is going to be well-known on the Last Day, no one was in need to ask, "Who is Muhammad?"

---

[23]That is, either in *ahadith* or in reports originating with the Companions and contemporaries of the Prophet.

[24]Place of worship, mosque.

They came and sat in front of him, and one of them said, "You are Muhammad."

The Prophet ﷺ replied, "Yes, I am Muhammad."

Then the second one said, "And you are Ahmad."[25]

And he said, "I am Ahmad, also.

The Prophet's names are written on all the *masjid's* walls in Medina, about 250 names, but the Naqshbandi Order knows one thousand names for the Prophet ﷺ—one thousand! To have many names is a sign of a person's honor; the more names there are for a person, the more honor it is for him. Therefore, he has been honored with one thousand names. As his name in Paradise is Abdul-Karim,[26] in Hells it is "Abdul-Qahhar,"[27] on the Divine Throne "Abdul-Majid,"[28] on earth "Muhammad," and in the Heavens "Ahmad".

They addressed him exactly as they knew, as "Ahmad" and "Muhammad". Then they asked him, "Could you tell us what is the greatest witnessing in the holy book that has come to you?"

Then at that time the angel Gabriel ﷺ came and brought the verse, *"Bismillahi-r-Rahmani-r-Rahim. Shahida-Llahu annahu la ilaha illa Hua, wal-malaikatu wa ulu-l-'ilmi qaiman bil-qist. La ilaha illa Hua-l-'Azizu-l-Hakim"*[29]— Gabriel just brought this verse to him and he recited it. Then those two priests fell upon his hands, upon his feet, also, saying, "You are that prophet about whom Moses informed us and about whom Jesus Christ gave good tidings. You are *that* prophet, and we are witnesses to that."

---

[25]The names "Muhammad" and "Ahmad" are both derived from the same three-letter root "h-m-d," denoting "the praised one."

[26]The Servant of the Noble or Honored One.

[27]The Servant of the Subduer.

[28]The Servant of the Most Generous.

[29]"In the name of Allah, the Most Beneficent, the Most Merciful. Allah [Himself] bears witness that there is no deity except Him, and [so do] the angels and those of knowledge, [that He is] maintaining [creation] in justice. There is no deity except Him, the Almighty, the Wise." (3:18)

Allah Almighty Himself is the Witness! Who can be greater than Him? He says, "I Myself am witness that I am the One, the Creator, the Lord of the worlds, the Lord of creatures, the Lord of the universe, the Lord of the Heavens, and I am that One besides whom no one may be able to do anything. I am that One who has eternal Power Oceans and eternal Knowledge and Wisdom Oceans with Myself," He Himself witnesses for Himself. "And also all angels, they are witnesses to My unity and My existence. And everyone who has been honored with knowledge, every learned and knowledgeable person, also says *'La ilaha illa-Llah,'* proclaiming My existence and My unity."

Therefore, Allah Almighty gives honor to the children of Adam by their saying *"La ilaha illa-Llah,"* by their proclaiming the existence of Allah Almighty and His unity. That is the honor that we have been given, and that is the knowledge from which all knowledge comes. It is the source of all knowledge and all wisdoms, and knowledge comes forth from that source to say, "There is no God but Allah. All power, absolute Power Oceans and absolute Wisdom Oceans, are for Him, Almighty Allah."

Therefore, at every time, people who want honor receive honor by proclaiming the existence and unity of their Lord, Allah Almighty. If a person does not proclaim the existence and unity of Allah Almighty, he is never given honor or knowledge or wisdom. Anyone who claims that he has wisdom and knowledge, he *must* proclaim the existence of God, Almighty Allah, and His unity. That verse is the greatest witness in the Holy Qur'an, and it includes everyone by saying *"ulu-l-'ilm,"* the people of knowledge. Those who have knowledge and wisdom, they are saying, *"La ilaha illa-Llah*, there is no God but Allah, Almighty Allah."

Now in our time, all nations are falling into crises. And we are seeing that in our time, like a new fashion, ideas are coming for denying the existence of the Lord, Almighty Allah, a new current from Satan. Satan and his helpers, his devils, are teaching people to deny the existence of the Lord, Allah Almighty. As the first step, they are teaching people to deny the existence of the Creator, and second, they are teaching them to claim that each one is the creator of himself, so that there are endless 'creators,' each one claiming that only *I* am in existence. They are denying the Creator, Allah

Almighty, and proclaiming their own lordship or godhood; anyone who has a little bit of authority is proclaiming his own lordship. That is a sign of darkness in the hearts of people, and it makes the future of mankind in this world dark and black. That is the reason that in our time most of the honor of mankind is taken away and you can find only very few honorable people.

Earlier there were a lot of honorable ones among people, but now a wrong system has come, wrong ideas which are saying that all people are equal. Now there is no respect for anyone because that current that is denying the existence of the Lord, Almighty Allah, is making people like a flock of sheep or goats. No respect for anyone! They are saying, "I am like you are." No respect for parents, no respect for holy men, no respect for old people—nothing. Yes, you can find millions, perhaps billions, of such people.

It means that honor and respect have been taken away from people, although earlier there were a lot of honorable people. And it began from the year 1789, the French Revolution, from that time when honorable people became the 'feet' and the 'feet' became the 'head'. Holy books are informing us about this through traditions.

This is not a good sign, and it is a fruit of *kufr*, unbelief. That tree that was planted in the French Revolution is now giving its fruits. All the crises in the world are coming from that tree, its fruits, and we are eating them, bitterly eating. People *must* eat them; it is a punishment.

This life is every day getting to be more bitter. Why? Because people are denying the existence of Allah Almighty and they are saying, "Only *we* are in existence, not anyone else." Therefore, we are advising people, as all prophets and their inheritors, *awliya*, advised the servants of God, Almighty Allah, to come and believe in the existence of Allah. *That* gives us honor, here and Hereafter. If we do not teach our children, do not look after their beliefs, then darkness will come on ourselves, also, and there will be no respect given to such people, here or Hereafter. ▲

6: steps to becoming free from our egos

Allah Almighty says, *"Wa khuliq al-insanu da'ifa,* Allah created man weak."[30]   It means that people need a covering, they need support; they need to be protected and defended, also, from enemies. Therefore, we are in need to have with ourselves something like an umbrella, to be under it in order to be in safety. We are in need of that here and on the Day of Resurrection.

Allah Almighty makes beliefs and faith to be an umbrella for everyone, protecting people here and Hereafter. In this world, during this life, everywhere, at every time, like rain, so many burdens are falling on people, raining heavily on them, so that without beliefs and faith you can't keep them away from yourself. Therefore, Allah Almighty makes faith and beliefs for His weak servants, to keep them, to protect them here and Hereafter.

Each day you may face so many things that are harming you and giving you trouble and suffering. If no beliefs, you can't carry it; this life is a heavy burden. Without believing in the Lord, Allah Almighty, it is impossible to carry it; so many people are unable to carry it and are killing themselves. But the one who believes in his Creator, in his Lord, Allah Almighty, and who believes in the eternal life, it is all right for him. That is an umbrella, giving a support to him to carry this life's heavy burden.

In our days, everywhere you are seeing that people are going down and each day their complaints are increasing. And each day, glory to Allah Almighty, you are hearing about something that was not in existence earlier; each day some new thing is coming out and going on. It is difficult to ex-

---

[30](4:28)

plain how in our time the sources of evil are increasing day by day, but it shows that heavenly occurrences are affecting people on earth. And we are seeing, also, that as long as people think that no relationship exists between earth and the Heavens, those troubles are increasing. We are observing that point.

People are saying that no relationship exists between earth and the Heavens. They are telling themselves that we are now free from every divine command or divine control; they are saying, "We are taking our freedom."

How can they say this, when divine commands have come to people through divine religions? But day by day, people are leaving divine commands and they are thinking, "We can do anything and we are free. No one can prevent us from doing anything that we like to do!" That is the idea, the new idea, of people.

Then, the Divine Controller says, "You are free. You may do anything, but you must know that punishment is always coming with you and running together with you. You are free to do, and *I* am free, also, to do anything to you, freely." That is the reason why each day crises and troubles and sufferings are increasing and not lessening.

People are thinking that economic conditions are the main reason for these crises. They are foolish people who are saying this; only no-mind people can say this, because we are observing the same crises in rich countries. If your country is not rich enough, I have been to one of the richest countries on earth, Switzerland, and I have seen that there, also, crises and depression are increasing among people. The more a person makes himself free from divine commands, the more he is going to be a slave to his ego, a servant and a slave to his ego's desires. And our ego's desires are endless. No matter how much you may run after it, to fulfill its desires, it is impossible to reach a limit. Therefore, even in rich countries, depression and crises are mounting.

What is the *dawa'*, cure, for it—*what is the cure?* Allah knows His servants; the one who made this tape recorder knows best how you can use it. Allah Almighty created man and He knows best how man must use his life.

Therefore I am saying that whoever wants to be free from divine commands, there must be something wrong in his head, and whoever thinks that crises are coming from economic problems, he is also an ignorant person, not knowing anything about mankind.

Allah Almighty knows our characteristics and, through the first prophet, Adam 𝕒, He made for man, for the children of Adam, *halal* and *haram*.[31] Those are boundaries, to put a limit on our desires. But our egos want to be free for everything, and that is the end of our life, that is destroying us!

Therefore, as we are weak and can easily be carried away by our egos and by Satan, we are in need to protect ourselves under an umbrella of faith. What is that faith? *You must believe in God, Almighty Allah, and you must keep the limits that He put for us, saying, "This you have permitted to take or to do, and that is prohibited for you."*

That puts a limit on our actions. If there are no limits in a religion, it is not a religion, it is not a faith. There *must* be limits. But now everyone wants to have a religion without putting any boundaries. That is the whole reason why people are going down, each day becoming worse, going from bad to worse, and from worse to worst, also.

We are in need to establish a shelter for ourselves in order to be in safety, and this is our shelter and umbrella: *to believe in God and to believe in the Last Day.* Therefore, each prophet called people to believe in Allah Almighty, the Creator, and to believe in the Last Day.

It is not enough to believe in God Almighty only, while not believing in the Last Day, not believing in Paradise and Hells, because, without belief in the eternal life, people are thinking that there is no responsibility for themselves. But "no responsibility" is for animals only. Human beings have responsibility, and that is the main point that Allah Almighty ordered to all the prophets: to proclaim that there is an eternal life, there is a judgment day.

---

[31] The permissible and the prohibited.

Everyone must be judged in the Divine Presence according to his actions during this life. *That* is responsibility. And without there being *halal* or *haram*, without there being some things which we are commanded to do and some others to leave, there is no responsibility.

We are carrying that responsibility. Therefore, everyone who has been ordered to do something or to leave off something is in need of strong will power to keep those orders. Without will power you can't do anything. Your will must be above your ego's desires so that you can command your ego to do something or to leave off something; without will power it is impossible. And without worshiping, it is impossible for a person to take his will power in his hands.

And among worships, there is no other worship like fasting for sharpening our will power. Fasting sharpens it to cut those egos' desires. Therefore, fasting is important in our lives so that we can command our egos.

Now we are fasting from *halal*, from permitted things. During Holy Ramadan we are fasting and leaving *halal* eating and drinking because Allah Almighty says to leave it. Then what about prohibited things? If you are leaving *halal*, you must be able to leave *haram*. And that is the benefit of fasting: you are sharpening your will power. If for this one month you may be able to take command of your ego, Allah Almighty may support you during the other eleven months; you may be able, at any time, to command your ego. But if you leave your ego free during this month, during Holy Ramadan, your ego will carry you during the other eleven months.

Therefore, we must try to fast and to practice after Ramadan, also. After Ramadan, fasting is *sunnah*, not *fard*.[32] The Prophet ﷺ made it a *sunnah* so that sometimes we may order ourselves to fast, to keep away from our egos' desires. Our egos are saying, "What about *that* fasting? It is not *fard!*" And you may answer it, "Yes, I know it is not *fard* but the Prophet said, 'You may fast,' and, as he fasted, therefore I must fast, also.'

---

[32]*Sunnah* refers to that which was practiced and recommended by the Prophet but not obligatory *(fard)*.

That *sunnah* fasting also gives us some will power. Therefore, the Prophet ﷺ taught us and made fasting on certain days *sunnah*, particularly six days after '*Eid*.[33] And during each month, when the moon becomes perfectly full, the thirteenth, fourteenth and fifteenth, the brightest days, may also be *sunnah* fasts. And for the second '*Eid*,[34] from the beginning of Dhul-Hijjah, nine days, or only the Day of 'Arafat; and in Muharram, also, ten days or two days or three days; and Rajab and Sha'ban, two holy months, also. Or during each month you may fast three days, or you may fast each week on Monday and Thursday, as you like.

This is *sunnah* in order to keep your ego under your control any time you may order it, and that day you may be in safety and you may feel a happiness within yourself, and Allah will support you. Therefore, it is a good habit to follow *sunnah* fasting. For every occasion [mentioned above], you may observe it. It gives us more power, more will power.

Fasting means to command and to keep your ego from any of its desires. Yes, it is fasting if your ego is asking for something to eat, to do, to say, and you say "No"; *that* is fasting, also. And fasting from evil keeps you under the shelter of your faith because, for every trouble that reaches and touches people, its only reason is that they are fulfilling some desire of their egos. Then, after fulfilling your ego's desire, you must expect that something will touch you and harm you.

It is impossible for a person to run after his ego's desires without some harm touching him. *It must be;* it is a divine judgment. '*Fa man ya'mal mithqala dharratin khairan yarah, wa man ya'mal mithqala dharratin sharran yarah*'[35]— whoever does even the smallest thing of good, he must keep that reward with himself, in his heart, and whoever does the smallest thing from the desires of his ego, some punishment must touch him. He must await it, he must expect it. Only if he asks forgiveness from his Lord, Allah Almighty,

---

[33]That is, six days in Shawwal, the Islamic month immediately following Ramadan.

[34]'*Eid al-Adha*, the Festival of Sacrifice, which falls on the tenth of the month of Dhul-Hijjah. The Day of 'Arafat is the ninth of Dhul-Hijjah.

[35]"Then whoever does an atom's weight of good shall see it, and whoever does an atom's weight of evil shall see it." (99:7)

saying, "O my Lord, I have made a mistake, forgive me," then that asking forgiveness carries that punishment away from him. Otherwise, it is impossible. The one who runs after his ego's desires must be punished.

And we are asking forgiveness from Allah Almighty for everything in which we are following the desires of our egos. As long as people are following their desires, there is not going to be a good future for humanity on earth and darkness is awaiting it. Therefore, all the prophets advised their nations to take a shelter.

I heard that in Switzerland that some people are building a house above the ground and another underground to be their shelter from atomic weapons. But they are *not* shelters. The shelter for people is only their belief, their faith. The stronger it is, the more suitable it is for keeping and protecting you, here and Hereafter.

People are afraid of fire, atomic fire or other fires. In the next life also there is fire, and the shelter from that fire is only our souls. Here people are afraid of fire falling on them from the skies, but on the Day of Resurrection, Hells will send out bombs of fire as big as houses, and every person will be protected only under the shelter of his faith. ▲

7: taking control of ourselves

May Allah Almighty keep us from falsehood! Every falsehood brings sufferings to people. Therefore, till all falsehood goes away from this earth, sufferings are never going to finish. And Allah Almighty sent His prophets to take away falsehood from the earth, and finally our Prophet, beloved Muhammad ﷺ, just came to take away all falsehood from the earth and to spread truth everywhere.

We are living at a time when, in the general view, falsehood is filling every place and truth is secret, hidden. And most people are working for falsehood. They may know it or not know it, but if they are not working for falsehood directly, they are working indirectly, each one putting one stone to build falsehood on earth, and they are imagining that that building will be a shelter for themselves. But all of those who are putting even one stone for falsehood and entering under it, that building will fall on them and finish them, taking them away.

It is important for every believer to control his actions, his deeds. Without looking after his actions, everyone is going to lose. And Satan knows everything concerning the life of mankind. He knows all the paths, and in each path he puts something from that falsehood. In every religion, Satan has put something from his secret traps; in every kind of thought, he has put some of his tricks.

Therefore, *tariqats*, Sufi orders, and in our time the Most Distinguished Naqshbandi Order, are ordering thought control to people. If you are able to make a control on your thoughts, you may be in safety from satanic ideas, but if someone is not able to control his thoughts, then satanic ideas and falsehood are coming into his mind through his thoughts.

If a person gets under the control of Satan, you can't say that he is an obedient servant to his Lord. And in our time, Satan is controlling almost all people's thoughts. He is controlling everyone, every community, every religion—claiming to control Islam, also, the last Message of Allah Almighty, wanting to take control of it. And in our time, I am sorry to say that Satan is controlling the thoughts of Muslims, also. A huge number of Muslims, their thoughts are just controlled by Satan. This is a reality; no doubt about it.

If Satan did not control the Muslim community, they must be the first on earth and their words must be listened to. But we are not the first. The Muslim world is only first from the end, not from the beginning; next to the last, all of it, because every level of Muslims, ignorant or learned people or scholars or statesmen, every level, every class of people, is controlled by Satan and satanic ideas—finished! Therefore we are not able to save ourselves from Satan's control.

While you are under his control, particularly while your thoughts are controlled by Satan, no hope for you to be an obedient servant to Allah Almighty. It is impossible. That thought of yours which is under satanic control will never let you be a sincere servant, an obedient servant and a beloved one in the Divine Presence. Therefore we are saying that almost all people are falling under satanic control in our time, and Satan is controlling the earth now, from East to West, from North to South, without doubt, and he has established his hegemony and kingdom on earth. You may know it or not. If you know, it is better than being ignorant about that satanic control.

That is the first thing that we must think about as Muslims and believers. You must control yourself. If you find any control by Satan on yourself, on your actions or on your thoughts, you must look after them to make them clean.

Now we are in the holy month, Ramadan, and we have been ordered to fast. Grandshaykhs say that there are three kinds of fasting, and the most important fasting is the third kind, making a control on your thoughts, and that is the fasting of prophets and saints. If anyone is not able to control his thoughts, it means that his heart is in the hands of Satan, and the heart is the *sultan* which commands our organs and our limbs. Otherwise, our limbs and organs would be under our hearts' command. Therefore, the most important kind of fasting is to control your thoughts while you are fasting.

This is a simple fasting that we are doing now, not eating or drinking. We are happy, also, in waiting for a good breakfast; that is our pleasure in fasting. This is the first level of fasting. But if you can try to guard your limbs, your organs, to make them fast, also, that is stronger than the first kind of fasting, so that you may be able to help your heart to take control of your thoughts, because as long as you are leaving your eyes without control, your ears without control, your tongue without control, to look, to say, to listen as they like, you will not be able to take control of your thoughts, since the source of thoughts comes through your eyes. This looking around is the source of thoughts in your heart. With no control on your looking, on your eyes, there is no control on your thoughts. You *must* fall down, and Satan is able to take control of your thoughts through your looking. Therefore, it is so important for the one who is fasting to try to take control of his eyes.

People are thinking that just not eating and drinking is enough for fasting, but it is really the lowest form of fasting. We are asking to make our minds safe, safe from satanic ideas, and our thoughts clean from satanic control, and this fasting helps us, from the beginning up to its perfection. Even if you are only fasting to keep yourself away from eating and drinking, it is helpful, it is the way to reach thought control. Without taking the first step, you can't reach the top step. Therefore, the one who wants to make himself in safety from satanic control must be careful about his fasting.

If you do not control your thoughts, your thoughts will push you or pull you into falsehood. They are not going to remain only as thoughts. Thoughts turn into actions—yes? And then we are going to be the servants or helpers of falsehood, to build Satan's kingdom. Without knowing or without thinking, we are working for Satan and his kingdom. Therefore, it is so important to take control of our thoughts.

Among *tariqats* we have some methods. If a person wants to keep his heart clean, Satan no longer controlling him, we have a method in our *tariqat*. One grandshaykh was ordering his *murids*,[36] when they were thinking bad thoughts related to this life, to take a shower bath.

If a person thinks about *haram*, he is ordered to take a shower, *ghusl*. Each time that *haram* thought comes and repeats in your heart, you are going to take a shower and then pray two *rak'ats*. Then Satan says, "It is useless if I give bad thoughts to this person because each time, he is getting up to take a shower and pray two *rak'ats*. It is not a good thing to make a person take a shower and pray. No benefit for me. *He* is gaining!" And if you continue with that method for forty days, then he will never come to you to take control of your thoughts, running away, because he will say, "We are gaining nothing, but *he* is gaining."

And even for beginners, they are asked to do *wudu*.[37] If you are thinking some bad things, Satan putting into your mind some bad thoughts or *harams*, then you may renew your *wudu* and make *Shahadah*[38] and *istighfar*.[39] Then Satan will say, "Each time, that person is making *wudu*, making *istighfar*, renewing his *Shahadah*. What am I doing? I am giving *him* benefit! I must leave him."

Yes, for everything there is something against it to protect believers from satanic ideas. Therefore, it is good manners to make *wudu* for every prayer or to take a shower, *ghusl*, once every twenty-four hours. It takes away bad thoughts from you, and day by day they are going to finish. If a person does not leave those bad thoughts that are in his heart, his name is written in the book of Satan; famous names are with Satan. And in our time, most people are doing things without thinking about controlling their minds, controlling their actions. But those uncontrolled minds and hearts

---

[36]Followers, disciples.

[37]The ablution preceding prayers.

[38]The Declaration of Faith, *"Ashhadu an la ilaha illa-Llah wa ashhadu anna Muhammadu Rasul-Allah,* I bear witness that there is no deity except Allah and I bear witness that Muhammad is Allah's Messenger."

[39]Asking for forgiveness.

are in the hands of Satan, and they are building on one side and destroying from the other side.

Allah Almighty likes good actions, but they must be clean actions. Clean actions are only going to be with clean thoughts. Otherwise, if you haven't clean thoughts, you are not going to do good actions or good activities. And in our days, Satan and his armies are claiming that they are taking each one of mankind, in the East and the West, in their hands, Satan saying, "In *my* hands! One hand of mine is in the East, one hand in the West, and I am commander over the children of Adam and controller of their thoughts."

Therefore, we are seeing that day by day satanic methods are increasing among people, satanic inventions are growing. If you sit down to think, you can't think, such things people are inventing! Originally, anything may be useful for beliefs, for goodness, for charity; but Satan never lets people use such new inventions for charity or for the benefit of the children of Adam, and they are preparing themselves to use every opportunity for the East to take away the West and for the West to take away the East. Nothing is useful for the children of Adam without there quickly coming another thing to harm them.

Therefore, we must be very careful in our steps and we must try to take control of ourselves. And if you are able to take control of your body, then, when Allah Almighty gives you an opportunity for your heart and your heart becomes stronger and able to keep your limbs and organs on a good path, at that time you will be an obedient servant.

Now we are hearing that a new disease is spreading and also that no one may be able to take it away. No cure for so many illnesses; it is not only one or two or three—also cancer; everywhere, with everyone. *That* disease is only going to appear in uncontrolled bodies. If a body is controlled, it is impossible for such an incurable disease to grow. Therefore, to take control of yourself gives you benefit physically and spiritually.

And we have an opportunity during Holy Ramadan more than at any other time. The one who is able to control himself during this Ramadan is going to be able, by Allah Almighty's support, to take control of himself for the other eleven months. Everything begins small and grows, good things and bad things, good habits and bad habits; for each one we have a beginning. And the beginning is difficult, but you must be patient and continue. If you know that something is right, you must continue to keep that way, even though it may be so difficult. Difficulties may be overcome by strong faith, and strong faith must always be with those people who are able to control themselves.

Allah Almighty gave us His messages through His prophets, and the summary of those messages is only to make people be able to take control of themselves. Therefore Allah Almighty orders prayers five times a day, plus *sunnah* worshipping, also. There are the five times of prayer which Allah Almighty makes obligatory, *fard*, on His servants, but the Prophet ﷺ did *sunnah* prayers in the daytime and the nighttime, also, so that those times of praying are always making a control on our limbs and on our hearts.

The Prophet ﷺ did so many *sunnah* prayers that if you keep them day and night, there is going to be perfect control on your ego, because, as long as you leave your ego free, it escapes, running away, and if your ego runs away, no more control on it. Some people are objecting, "Why five times a day?" but they are ignorant people. They do not understand what are the divine wisdoms in making a lot of worshipping in a day, when so much worshipping always makes a strong control on ourselves, on our organs and on our limbs, and then on our thoughts.

It is a good opportunity for everyone to look after his *nafs*, after his ego, what it is doing and what it is ordering, particularly during this holy month. And at every time, we are asking forgiveness from Allah Almighty for our bad thoughts, and asking to make our hearts clean from dirty thoughts.

When they are going to be clean, then you will go to the station of *awliya*, who are still living everywhere on earth, although mostly they are hidden in our time; they may meet with us but we do not know who they are. And they are following the ways of the prophets by controlling every action of their limbs and organs, and controlling their thoughts. Therefore, more than anything, *tariqats* are teaching people to look after their hearts because hearts are the sources of goodness and badness. And we are asking from our Lord to guard our hearts and to help us to control our thoughts and actions. ▲

8: takınc care to make your lord pleased with you

Everyone must ask how we can make our Lord, Allah Almighty, pleased with us; everyone must ask about that point, how I may be able to make my Lord pleased with me. The one who can make his Lord pleased with him, he has reached the main goal here and Hereafter.

If you can't make your Lord pleased with you, what are you doing? Why are you alive, what is the meaning of your life? It is nonsense! Therefore, for so many people, to be inside the earth is better for them than to be on the face of it. And everyone must look at himself, whether to be inside this earth is better for him or whether to be on it is better; everyone must ask this question and must look for an answer from himself to himself.

Each day, each morning, we are awakening. Each night Allah Almighty is taking our souls temporarily, and our souls are returning to their homeland, to the Heavens, Allah Almighty permitting them to be free from this prison. Our bodies are prisons for our souls; when we are sleeping, they are getting their freedom and returning to their homeland. And, according to traditions, if a person sleeps *taher*, clean, then his soul reaches up to the Divine Throne, making *sajdah*,[40] worshipping, till that person awakes. If he does not sleep *taher*, it also gets to the Heavens but it is imprisoned in a dark place till that person awakes and it comes back to him. Therefore, when the one who sleeps clean awakens, he feels lightness; if not, he feels a heavy burden on himself. So each night, you must look to yourself.

And each morning when you are awakening, you are beginning a journey, traveling on earth. So many steps—going, coming, going, coming; you

---

[40]Prostration.

are going a long way each day. If you put your steps in a straight line, perhaps you would reach ten miles', twenty miles' distance, or more.

We are running, each day, but no one is asking to understand for what we are running, to where we are running, or which thing we are intending to reach. It is a long journey, each day. Everyone runs and tires, works and tires, but if you ask for what that is, people may say, "This is only for my provision, to eat and drink." And the pubs are waiting for them, the whole day working like robots, and each night, after finishing, those pubs are waiting for them, to go there and be there up to midnight. And they are living without asking what is the meaning of this life.

Each one of us must think at nighttime whether today I did something that made my Lord pleased with me. If he can say within his conscience that I did some good things or that I did my best with my Lord and with His servants, then he may know that to be on the earth is better for him than to be under the earth. Otherwise, to be under the earth is better for him than to be on it because each day he is carrying more responsibility and a heavier burden on himself. If he is not making his Lord pleased with him, to be in this life is nonsense for him. And if we do not reach that point during our life, it is difficult to make our Lord pleased with us after death.

A grandshaykh sent his *murid* to a cemetery and ordered him, "Go and stand in the middle of it. Go to the middle of the cemetery and call, 'O people lying in this cemetery, listen to me!'"

They can hear but they can't answer. Sometimes they can look and see, but at any time, if a person goes to a cemetery and says, "*As-salamu 'alaikum, ya ahla-l-qubur*, peace be on you, O people of the graveyard," they hear him. The one who is from the people of Paradise answers, receiving our *salam*, our greeting; the one who isn't does not reply but he hears it.

Now it is the holy month, and each day they can look at their visitors, also. During Ramadan, each day, each night, they can hear and see anyone who comes to visit them. After Ramadan, only each Thursday and Friday until Saturday morning's sunrise, for two complete days, they can see their visitors and hear their *salams* and their prayers for them, but during Holy

Ramadan it is always open. Therefore, it is important for living people to visit cemeteries from time to time, Allah Almighty permitting them.

You may pass through cemeteries in Europe, also. As I have been ordered, when I pass through cemeteries, I say *"La ilaha illa-Llah"* three times, saying also, *"Muhammadu Rasul-Allah, salla-Llahu 'alayhi wa sallam,"*[41] and calling, "O people who are lying in this graveyard, you who accepted, even at the last moment of your lives, and said *'La ilaha illa-Llah'* and passed away on that holy word, *as-salamu 'alaikum!"* Then you may recite a *Fatehah*[42] for those who may be in that graveyard of those people who said the holy word, *"La ilaha illa-Llah, Muhammadu Rasul-Allah, salla-Llahu 'alayhi wa sallam,"* even at the last moment, and if none of them is there, it may go to another cemetery in which there may be one or two or more.

At the least, *at the least,* you say *"La ilaha illa-Llah"* when you pass through that cemetery. That is a holy word which all the prophets said, from the beginning up to the end, and it is written on the Divine Throne, *"La ilaha illa-Llah,* there is no God but Allah." And after *"La ilaha illa-Llah,"* as we are looking and seeing and knowing, there is written *"Muhammadu Rasul-Allah, salla-Llahu 'alayhi wa sallam*—Muhammad is His Messenger," the Seal of the Prophets. In every cemetery that saying gives refreshment; yes.

Then that shaykh ordered his *murid* to go and stand in the middle of that cemetery and ordered him to ask, "O people who are lying in this cemetery, what do you want, what is your wish?" And as he had ordered, that *murid* went and asked it.

Allah Almighty can do anything! You must believe that the Lord of the Heavens can do anything—yes. The people lying in that graveyard, they were listening. Then Allah Almighty gave them permission to answer that *murid's* question.

---

[41]"Muhammad is the Messenger of Allah, Allah's peace and blessings be upon him."

[42]The first chapter *(surah)* of the Qur'an. It is an Islamic tradition to recite this *surah* for the dead.

The one who makes his Lord pleased with him, Allah Almighty grants him miracles, giving them to His servant. If you are a sincere and obedient servant, He grants to you miracles from His endless favors. And that shaykh was from those beloved people and an obedient servant to his Lord, and he was teaching his *murid*, and teaching ourselves and teaching all mankind.

Then Allah Almighty permitted those people in that graveyard to answer. They answered there, saying, "O our Lord's servant, O *'abd-Allah*! Our only wish, our only desire, is that we are asking from our Lord to give us one hour or even one minute of your life."

Why were they asking for a part of his life? To teach him the value of his life, to teach him that he was spending it, as we are spending *our* lives, leaving them without value. Yes. "Our desire is only to be given one hour from your life to make our Lord, during that hour, pleased with us.

"Because we are lying here, we can never think of making our Lord pleased with ourselves. We spent our lives uselessly, and now we are understanding what is the value of the life on earth. Therefore, all of us, our Lord's servants, we are asking from our Lord to give us one hour from your life, and we hope to make our Lord pleased with us during that hour." *That* was their desire.

All people in cemeteries would say this if they could speak and we could hear. We are doing *israf*, wasting our precious, precious lives. If people who are lying in cemeteries had all the treasures, all the gold on earth and under the earth, also, they would be ready to give it all if the Lord, Almighty Allah, were to ask payment for that minute or that hour; if they had all treasures, they would be ready to pay them all for one moment of life. But we do not know; we are heedless still. We never know what is the value of this moment's breaths, of even one breath. They would give all treasures to say only once *"La ilaha illa-Llah,"* but finished—breath finished, everything finished!

Therefore, it is a very, very great opportunity for ourselves to know the value of our breaths. People may *know* something but they have no certainty and then they can do nothing. So many people are reading books and knowing about religion or about Paradise and Hells, about the Day of Resurrection, but no praying, no worshipping, doing nothing for their Lord. A person may *know*, but the important knowledge is the knowledge of certainty which pushes you to worship, which gives you the power to worship, to be an obedient servant of your Lord. Therefore, the important thing is to know and to obtain certainty for our knowledge. And from where can you obtain that certainty?

Once the Prophet ﷺ asked a *sahabi*, one of his Companions, "*Kaifa as-baht*—how did you awaken today?"

He said, "O *Rasul-Allah*, O Messenger of God, Allah Almighty, I awoke and came to this day *muminan*, as a believer."

Then the Prophet asked him, "What is the sign of your faith?"

And he said, "O Messenger of God, Almighty Allah, I was in the situation of seeing the Day of Resurrection, the place of Judgment Day, which will be in Damascus; I saw it. People were gathering, a huge crowd of people from the beginning up to the end, crowded on that Plain of *Mahshar*. And I saw at my right hand Paradise and at my left hand Hells, and I put my foot on the Bridge that everyone must pass over"; if passing, entering Paradise. "I saw the Scale, also, for weighing people's actions, worshipping and goodness."

Then the Prophet said, "That is correct, the true sign of your faith. It is right. Keep yourself on it."

That is certainty—*to know something exactly*. Otherwise, anyone can read but he does not reach that certainty; it is not enough for him to say it himself. And now we are also asking certainty from Allah Almighty concerning the value of our lives.

The people of the graveyard, they had reached that certainty because the veils had been taken away from their hearts' eyes. Then they were able to look and see what is unseen to us now, and they *knew*, asking for one hour's time from that *murid's* life to be given to them so that they could make their Lord pleased with them. That was their only aim. They were not asking to come to this life to do business; finished—all business had been put aside. Yes, *nothing!* Their only desire was to make their Lord pleased with them.

Now *we* have that opportunity, everyone. We must try at every time to make our Lord pleased with us. And the way, the only way, is that you must think before every action—think whether it is something that makes my Lord pleased with me or not. *Only this we must ask ourselves.*

I am sitting here; I am speaking and you are listening. If this activity of ours makes our Lord pleased with us, if our conscience says, "Yes, it is all right, it is something that makes your Lord pleased with you," then you must do that.

This is only an example, but for everything that you want to do, think about it a little bit. If your conscience signals that it is all right, that now your Lord is looking at you and He is going to be pleased with you, you may do it. And if you are in doubt about it, there is another method you may use:

For every action that you want to do, you must say *'Bismillahi-r-Rahmani-r-Rahim.'*[43] It means, "O my Lord, I am doing this for Your Divine Pleasure." If you can say *"Bismillahi-r-Rahmani-r-Rahim"* for that action, it is all right; you may do it. It makes your Lord pleased with you and makes *you* pleased, also, here and Hereafter. ▲

---

[43]In the name of Allah, the Most Beneficent, the Most Merciful.

9: the importance of experiencing hunger

Grandshaykh was saying that every way is now closed, locked, but one way, to say for every action *"Bismillahi-r-Rahmani-r-Rahim,"* opens every locked door. You can use it as much as you want. No matter how much you may say it, it is all right, it is not going to be too much. Say, always, *"Bismillahi-r-Rahmani-r-Rahim."*

When a servant says *"Bismillahi-r-Rahmani-r-Rahim,"* he makes himself non-existent, considering himself nothing. *"Wa khuliqa-l-insanu da'ifa".*[44] Allah Almighty says that I created man weak, and if He says he is weak, he *is* weak; he can't be powerful. Yes, weak, and we are in need of help. And each time the one who thinks or knows that he is weak says *"Bismillahi r-Rahman ar-Rahim,"* it means, "O my Lord, I am nothing. I can't do anything if You do not support me or help me; *I can't do anything.* And I am saying, *'Bismillahi-r-Rahmani-r-Rahim.'* By Your power I may do; by Your power I may live; by Your power I may do everything, every difficult thing." All difficulties are going to be made easy by saying *"Bismillahi-r-Rahmani-r-Rahim."*

A good tidings for fasting people! Grandshaykh was saying that when a person is hungry, Allah likes him. Allah Almighty never likes someone to be full of food, but when he has an empty stomach He likes him because *He* never eats, never drinks. If He didn't like that being hungry, He

---

[44](4:28)

wouldn't have allowed His Prophet to be hungry and to put a stone on his stomach.[45]

One day some *sahabah*, the Prophet's Companions, were saying to him, "O *Rasul-Allah*, we are tying stones onto our stomachs from hunger." Then the Prophet did like this and showed them the *two* stones he had put.

If it wasn't useful for building personalities, Allah Almighty would never have let them be hungry. From hunger no harm comes, but from eating harm comes to people. When a person is hungry, his heart opens, and when it opens, blood runs everywhere easily. No pressure on the heart from hunger; instead, it makes the heart to open. Its outward part opens, and also it opens within itself. When you are hungry, wisdom's sources open in your heart. When you are full, that closes.

Therefore, Allah Almighty made the *sahabah*, the Companions of the Holy Prophet, to be hungry from time to time, and the Prophet ﷺ was also hungry, because hunger makes a good personality. Everything affects the personality but hunger has the most effect on our personalities. Therefore, the *sahabah* were mostly hungry, or, if they were fasting, they might find only dates, one or three, eating very little. But that hunger established Islam in their hearts, establishing *iman*, faith, also. And they were such strong people, both physically and spiritually, because the less you eat, the more the physical body takes power. People who eat too much become weaker and weaker, and carriers of flesh.

Now, one most important point on which Grandshaykh was speaking: We are in need of faith, *iman*—yes? Faith may be imitation or it may be real, and we are in need of *real* faith, not imitation, only saying it with our lips. Everyone is in need of real faith. If we haven't real faith, at the last moment Satan may carry it away and leave a person without faith.

---

[45]Referring to the period known as the Boycott, during which the pagan Quraysh confined the Prophet and the Muslims to a locality in Mecca. There, while being hungry to the point of starvation due to the shortage of food, the Prophet and his Companions would tie stones to their stomachs to still the pangs of hunger.

We are in need of faith that controls our whole body, its inner side and its outer. That is important, and that is what Allah Almighty is asking from His servants—real faith. And our Grandshaykh, may Allah bless him, was giving a description of how real faith is going to enter into our hearts, and it is very important to know.

We have been ordered, as believers, to believe in what is real. *"Ya ay-yuha-l-ladhina amanu, aminu bil-Lahi wa rasulihi wal-kitabi-l-ladhi nazzala 'ala ra-sulihi.''*[46] Here, Allah Almighty is saying *"Ya ayyuha-l-ladhina amanu,"* address-ing the believers and commanding them to believe. That means, "O believ-ers by imitation, you must *really* believe in God or in the Lord, Allah Al-mighty, and you must believe in His Prophet and you must believe in His Book." And the important point is *how* we can believe or how we can ob-tain real faith.

That is an important point. You may ask this, but how can you find an answer? *You can find the answer through people who have reached real faith.* They know the way; others can't know that way. And Grandshaykh was saying, "If Allah Almighty wants to put real faith into the heart of a servant, He looks at his heart." Why? Because the dwelling-place or station of faith is the heart, and He looks *there*. If the conditions which Allah Almighty wants are right in your heart, He gives that real faith to your heart.

What are those conditions? What is Allah Almighty looking for in our hearts? Grandshaykh was saying that when every enjoyment of this world is taken away from your heart, then it is ready to be the station of real faith. If He sees that in your heart you are still putting somewhere enjoyment of this life, of *dunya, hubb-d-dunya*, love of this life, of this world—if He looks and sees a little bit, even from one side, He never gives, because it is dirti-ness to put the love of this life, of this world, into a heart that belongs to the Lord, Allah Almighty. It is dirty, dirtiness!

You know (ladies more than gentlemen know) that if you put milk into a pot in which there is a little bit of dirtiness, it is going to be sour. There-

---

[46]"O you who believe, believe in Allah and His Messenger and the Book that He sent down to His Messenger." (4:136)

fore, don't say, "What does it matter if there is a little bit of enjoyment of this life in our hearts? If we keep it there, what does it matter?"

No! During the Night Journey,[47] the angel Gabriel ﷺ brought to the Prophet, Sayyidina Muhammad ﷺ, wine in one pot and milk in another pot, saying, "You may choose one of these." He chose milk, and Gabriel said, "You have chosen the one of *fitrah*, nature."

That means that milk makes the physical body grow. That is nature, suitable for nature. And milk also represents *fitrat al-Islam*, the nature of Islam. Wine, no; wine destroys. Therefore, he chose milk. And as milk is destroyed, soured, by a small amount of dirtiness in a pot, so our hearts are a pot for faith, and a little bit of dirtiness from this world makes our faith sour.

Therefore, Allah Almighty is looking. When you are going to be finished with this world's enjoyment, then it may be put in there, Allah Almighty giving you real faith. Don't be foolish and say, "How can I leave the enjoyment of this life?" *Do you know, when real faith gets into your heart, what kind of enjoyment you will feel—do you know that?* If you do not know, don't say, "How can I leave my enjoyment? I am enjoying a little bit during this life, I am still looking around and enjoying." But what are you going to enjoy in prison?

You are in prison. What is enjoyment in prison? But real faith takes you out of prison, taking you from darkness to the lighted Heavens. Such a person may put one foot on earth and the other he may put in the Heavens, being free for everything. Now you are in prison, but when that real faith enters, you will not be in need to ask enjoyment from this dirty world. It is the 'toilet' for the other, that great world; yes. What enjoyment can you have in the toilet? *Nothing!*

Awliya, they know the hidden wisdoms, secret wisdoms, for everything. I am not saying that a person may reach that level in one step; that

---

[47]The Prophet's miraculous journey from Mecca to Jerusalem, and then to the Heavens and the Divine Presence of his Lord.

may be only for *awliya*. But it is possible to take away from your heart, little by little, the enjoyment of this life.

You may speak and address your ego or yourself directly: "We are in this world but we are not here for playing. Playing is for little boys. But you, O Thomas, or Nicholas, or 'Ali," you must say to yourself, "up to where are you going to play? No limit for you for that playing? When are you going to return to Reality?"

And little by little, you will take your foot away from those enjoyments, moving it to Enjoyment Oceans through real faith. A little bit at a time; each time, you may put it less, less, less. Then you are going to be a person who may eat, may drink, but only to live; you are not going to be a person who lives only for eating and drinking.

You must understand these two ways. Most people live only for eating and drinking. Then what is the difference between themselves and animals? *They* live only for eating and drinking, and if a person lives for eating and drinking, no difference between himself and animals. Therefore we are saying that the Prophet and his Companions were taking less to eat and drink because they were in need of it only to live.

You may understand in which class you may be of the two classes. Are you living for eating and drinking only? Then you must put yourself in the zoo. But if you are eating and drinking to live, you may be a distinguished one among people, and you may balance yourself, also. Then you are with the Prophet and his Companions, and that makes you, step by step, come into the station of real faith and opens your heart to real faith.

And we are asking forgiveness. This is an important lecture that we are in need of: that in *tariqats* we are making a limit for enjoyment, even of *halal,* so that the followers of *tariqats,* and particularly the followers of the Naqshbandi *Tariqat,* may step into the area of real faith. ▲

10: cleaning your heart from the love of this life

For real faith, we are in need to know about *Akhirah*, the Hereafter. We must know, because as long as our hearts are occupied with this world, it is difficult for real faith to make room in our hearts.

The Prophet, beloved Muhammad ﷺ, was saying, *"Kulla yawmin la az-dad fihi 'ilma yuqaribni il-Allahi ta'ala fa la burika li fi tulu' shamsi dhalika al-yawm;* if a day comes in which I do not increase in divine knowledge, it is not a blessed day for me." Yes; when the Prophet ﷺ says that each day must be more than the day before it in divine knowledge, it is an important rule for everyone.

If we increase in something for this life, that is nothing, but rather we must increase each day in *ma'rifat*, divine knowledge. And it is a part of divine knowledge, perhaps an obligatory part, for every believer to know about the Hereafter, as a person who wants to go to *Hajj*, pilgrimage, asks about Jiddah, Mecca Mukarramah and Madinah Munawwarah[48] because he intends to make *Hajj* and is in need to know. As much as he can know about Hijaz, he tries to learn.

Then what about if we believe in eternal life, the life hereafter, and each day we are coming closer to the life hereafter or to eternal life—is it not necessary to ask about that life and about the Hereafter? It is a part of divine knowledge to learn and to know, day by day increasing in knowledge.

What is the benefit of increasing in that knowledge? We may mention two kinds of benefits when you increase in that knowledge about the life in

---

[48]Jiddah, Mecca and Medina, the three main cities of Hijaz, in which pilgrims stay or pass through during the *Hajj*.

the Hereafter. The first of them is that our hearts, little by little, get to be in contact with the eternal life and its conditions. We are taking our heart from this temporary life's conditions and enjoyments, taking it to the eternal life's conditions and enjoyments. And that is important, because the Prophet 鬘 said that the most dangerous thing or thought for a believer is to have in his heart the love of this life.

The love of this life is the source of every sin. *"Hubb ad-dunya rasu kulli khatiyah;* every evil has its source in the love of this life."* Through that love devils may be able to control our thoughts and to put their hands into our hearts and take us toward evils. Therefore the Prophet 鬘 said that it is the most dangerous thing for believers to have their hearts attached to this life's pleasures and its love.

Yes. We have been ordered to take from this life only what is enough for ourselves, because if it is more and more, it is going to be more of a burden on ourselves, preventing us from moving toward Allah Almighty, like a person putting big iron balls-and-chains on his feet; then he can move only with too much difficulty. It begins with little balls; then, the more our property, our *dunya,* increases, that ball is also going to be bigger and bigger and bigger, and then you are going to be like an ant beside that huge iron ball. If it comes on you, it flattens you out.

Therefore, the advice of all the prophets is that you must take only that thing which you are in need of. Leave more for everyone else so that you may be free for walking toward Allah Almighty, because He is waiting for you.

That knowledge is the most necessary knowledge for everyone to know about the life of the Hereafter. It makes us free from this heavily-burdened life's conditions and makes our hearts also free for the love of Allah Almighty, for divine love. *You must be only for the love of your Lord, Allah Almighty!* Don't put a partner with Him—no partner, because Allah Almighty never likes to have a partner with Himself, and this life, this world, *dunya,* becomes a partner for the love, the divine love, of your Lord Almighty.

When you increase in the love of the permanent life, the eternal life, then Allah Almighty gives to your heart from His Divine Lights and darkness goes away, because the more the love of this life gets into your heart, the more darkness gets in, also. In darkness, all bad thoughts and fears grow, and dissatisfaction and unhappiness grow in your heart, because darkness makes them grow, but if darkness goes away from your heart, then it is lighted everywhere. No more troubles or unhappiness can be in your heart. Lights, Divine Lights, give you satisfaction and peace, and the more those lights grow in your heart, the more peace and happiness and satisfaction will grow in your heart, and hope will grow each day. That is the aim of the *hadith* of the Prophet ﷺ, when he asked to increase each day in divine knowledge about the eternal life and about the Lord, Allah Almighty. That gives more lights to your heart, and each day more satisfaction, more peace comes into your heart, and each day more pleasure.

Prophets and their followers—saints, *awliya*—are each day more joyful. They find in themselves more pleasure each day for the reason that they know that now they are approaching the Divine Presence of their Lord. Each one of the Prophet's Companions knew, and also every *wali*, saint, knows when he is going to leave this life. When they are going to die, they know, and every person of real faith also knows the day of his death.

Bilal, may Allah bless him, a *sahabi*, Companion of the Holy Prophet ﷺ, knew that he was going to die the next day, and the day before that and the week before, also, he was so happy. People around him were crying but he was very happy, very pleased and joyful, saying, "Oh-h! Tomorrow I will meet with my beloved Muhammad ﷺ and with his beloved Companions."

And all saints are asking for the day when they are going to meet their Lord, their Prophet, and his beloved Companions. One king-sized *wali*, Maulana Jalaluddin Rumi, may Allah bless him, ordered that the night he died should be like a wedding night for him, and he ordered that no one should cry or be sad. Have you seen a wedding at which the person is going to his wedding night and the people around him cry? No, very happy on that night! For what? "Because I am going to meet my beloved Lord, Allah Almighty, whom I love, for whose divine love my life has been lived;

I am going to meet *Him*. Why are *you* sad? I am so happy and joyful; then why are *you* crying? I don't like this," he was saying. And each one of those whose hearts are for their Lord and whose hearts are full-up with their Lord's love, they never look at this life and its enjoyments; no taste for anything from this life. Their physical bodies have needs for eating and drinking and procreation but they are not tasting that. They know what is the reality of this life, and they know about the life of the Hereafter in Paradise, and they know what is the Divine Presence.

If you say that there is beauty on earth, it is only that one drop which, if you put a needle in an ocean, the needle takes from that ocean, a little drop. All the beauty that this world and people have been given, it is only that drop, that little drop, from the endless Beauty Oceans of our Lord. *They* know about absolute Divine Oceans, about Mercy Oceans, about Beauty Oceans, about Power Oceans, about Wisdom Oceans, about endless Knowledge Oceans; *they know*. What thirsty person can take anything from one drop? They are asking to sink into those Oceans, and Allah Almighty is calling them, "O people, come to Me! Give your love to Me, not to anyone else. Nothing is suitable for your love except Me. Give it to *Me*!"

Therefore, we are in need of more knowledge each day so that we may increase in the knowledge of the eternal life, and when this life's pleasures are going to go away, then Allah Almighty gives instead those pleasures from among His Divine Pleasures. Don't suppose that if you do not look at this world's pleasures He leaves you without pleasures; no. He gives another kind of pleasure, real pleasure. This is an imitation life, it is not real life, and those who understand this, they are running after real life, real pleasure, real Beauty Oceans, to be *there*.

This is one benefit for the one who understands the real life and its pleasures, so that he begins to ask for more and to run after it. And the second benefit is that then you will leave every badness, you will leave devils' ways and their advice. You will see them as dirty and you will say to yourself, "Don't touch them. Leave them alone!"

If you have been asked to leave permitted, *halal,* enjoyment little by little to be with divine enjoyment, then what about *haram* enjoyments, for which all devils are doing advertising? Yes, advertising! Now all devils are advertising for *haram*, for every forbidden thing, as Satan advertised the Forbidden Tree to Adam 舧 in Paradise. He said, "Oh, this is very good. You must eat. If you eat from this, you will never go out of Paradise."

He was the first advertiser, Satan, and he cheated Adam and Eve. (The first to believe in that advertisement was a woman; they are quickly accepting that. Hawwa, Eve, was saying that this must be a very good thing because the Advertiser is saying such a thing about this tree.) And now Satan and his armies from *ins wal-jinn*[49] are all advertisers for *haram*, for forbidden things. How can you be in safety now in our time?

It is so difficult, and the Prophet 舧 said that there will come a time on my nation, on my *ummah*, when to keep their faith will be more difficult than keeping fire in their hands; yes. Every place you go is full-up with advertisers for forbidden things, and if you are not supported by divine knowledge that makes clear to you the eternal life and its pleasures, it is too difficult to save yourself from these advertisers, from Satan and his volunteers. ▲

---

[49]From among mankind and jinn.

11: standing against our egos

We must try to know about our Lord, *ma'rifat-Allah*,[50] and the way passes through knowing yourself. Then you may find a way to the knowledge of Allah Almighty, divine knowledge.

As long as you are interested in this world and everything about it, you are going to be heedless of yourself, and people now are just occupied with everything that is around themselves. We must cut, little by little, step by step, our interest in what is around us, to turn our interest to ourselves.

We know about this life, *adh-dhahira-l-hayata-d-dunya*,[51] outward knowledge; we know about this world. But we do not know what is the wisdom for this planet—why, amidst a huge universe, this is the only living planet. To the One who made it and gave our life conditions on this planet, there must be not only one but perhaps so many wisdoms for this planet's being a living planet. But we are always using material eyeglasses to look at it and never using our hearts to understand what is the wisdom or wisdoms for this planet, which is for the children of Adam.

It is only a very small part of this universe, and the universe is of two kinds of materials. One, as we see, is this world and the skies. But there is another universe which is not the same kind as this universe, and it is impossible for the children of Adam to look at that universe with their physical bodies.

But we have been given an authority by the Creator, by Allah Almighty, to look at everything in existence that He has created. And we

---

[50]The inner knowledge of Allah the Exalted.
[51]The externals of the life of this world.

have, in Islamic mysticism, *tasawwuf*, a rule: it is impossible to know the Creator or to find a way to divine knowledge without knowing His creatures. If you do not know about this [tape recorder], how can you claim to find a way to its inventor?

Therefore, whoever wants to find a way to divine knowledge of the Lord, Allah Almighty, first he must know His creatures, every kind of creature in existence. Then he may find a way. Otherwise, it is impossible to leave something unknown from among His creatures and to ask to know about the Creator. And mankind, or the children of Adam, have been created and granted an authority and capability or ability to know everything in existence, to make everyone surrounding or encircling them under their authority.[52]

Yes, we have been given that, because, among all creatures, Allah Almighty only made mankind to be deputies for Himself. When a person is going to be a deputy for the Lord, Allah Almighty, he is granted such spiritual or divine powers that give him an authority to look at everything in existence; otherwise he is not a deputy. But we are still candidates for that, as 'Abdur-Rahim is a candidate to be an adult—yes, to be a father, but now he is a candidate. And we, also, all mankind, all the children of Adam, are candidates to be deputies, real deputies, if we leave off imitation and walk into the reality of being a deputy.

Allah Almighty sent prophets, peace be upon them, and He addressed one of those prophets, saying, "O My prophet, be enemy to your *nafs*. You must be against your ego because it is that one which is against Me. Be against your ego because it is the one, the single one among all creatures, which goes against Me." That is what is not allowing us to reach that real deputy's station, always staying on earth, not reaching our heavenly, real deputies' stations in the Divine Presence.

Allah Almighty was addressing one prophet, and if He is addressing

---

[52]As mentioned in the verse, "He has subjected to you [mankind] whatever is in the Heavens and whatever is on earth, all from Him. Indeed, in that are signs for a people who reflect." (45:13)

one, it means it is for all. And if all the prophets have been ordered to be against their egos, then what about ourselves?

Whoever is in agreement with his ego goes against his Lord, and whoever goes against his ego, he is going to be with his Lord, always agreeing. And it is impossible for a person to take all authority in existence as a real deputy until he is going to be *absolutely* against his ego. If he sometimes goes with his ego—even if he is mostly against it but *sometimes* with his ego—it is impossible for him to reach that real deputy's station. And every message that has come from Allah Almighty to His servants is, "O My servants, if you are claiming to be My servants, you must be against your egos. If you are not against your ego, you can't be My servant. Your ego will pull you to itself."

Therefore, we may summarize all the messages of the messengers of Allah Almighty, which are saying to people, "O people, you must be against your egos." The first sin was done for our ego. Our ego went against the order, the holy command, of Allah Almighty, and then Adam and Eve came down from Paradise onto the earth. The one who goes against the Lord's Will must be punished, and there is no punishment for you or for anyone until he goes against his Lord, nor any happiness or peace or success or honor for a person until he is going to be against his ego.

When Adam went against his Lord's command, quickly punishment came to him and made him come on earth. He cried for three hundred years in Serendib;[53] all his tears flowed down, becoming precious stones.[54] He was so angry with his ego and stood against it, and when he turned against his ego, Allah Almighty opened Paradise to him: "To you and your followers, those who are against their egos, this Paradise is open to them. They are still in prison. I am imprisoning you and your descendants on this planet, but you may get out of that prison by My Divine Authority."

---

[53]According to Islamic tradition, when Adam ﷺ was expelled from Paradise for disobeying Allah's command, he came to earth in Serendib, Ceylon, now known as Sri Lanka.

[54]Shaykh Nazim adds parenthetically, "It is precious when these tears come for the sake of Allah. *That* is precious, not for anything else."

One prophet, Sayyidina Yusuf, Joseph 舀, was in prison in Egypt, and that prison was the worst prison on earth. No one entered it and came out alive or without losing his mind, but he entered and for more than forty years he lived there and came out safe in his mind and body. Nothing was lacking, perfect. Why? He was in prison, but he had been given divine authority by his Lord, Almighty Allah, and he was free throughout the entire universe and was permitted to be in the Divine Presence, not in prison.

Therefore, if anyone is able to imprison his ego, Allah Almighty gives to him an authority through his soul, and he is free to be in East and West, or on earth or in the Heavens—to be one, to be one hundred, to be one thousand; yes, to be 124,000. He may be even more than that, 700,000. If there may appear now in our time a person who is able to be against his ego and to put it in prison, he may be given 700,000. As we are taking from this one physical body, it may be in 700,000 forms, its source coming from our spiritual power, looking and listening and speaking and able to do everything.

That is a dress of Paradise. Therefore, you must know about the life of the Hereafter so that this life becomes small and pleasure in this life is going to be, in front of that huge light, a small thing. The more this life becomes small in your eyes, the more the life in Paradise becomes bigger.

That is a dress in which Allah Almighty clothes His sincere servants. It begins by being seven, up to 700,000 now in our time, that dressing of Paradise, and in Paradise you can't say how many there are going to be for you. In this way, the real deputies are clothed from Paradise, a divine dress.

When I say "a divine dress," it means that Allah Almighty clothes them in His Divine Attributes, and no one can give a limit for the Divine Attributes. Everyone who is His real deputy, Allah Almighty clothes him in His Divine Attributes. At that time you are going to be a real deputy; when you are clothed in them—finished! *'Wa sakhkhara lakum ma fis-samawati wa ma fil-ardi jami'an'*[55]—that is the verse which shows that station for our-

---

[55] 45:13, whose translation is given in footnote 52.

selves. We have been given that power, that authority, to be in the entire universe.

And the way on which we are marching to reach that authority is only one, as Allah Almighty advised His prophet, saying, "Be against your ego," and no need for anything else. "When you are going to be against your ego, it will be all right. You may come to Me. Because your ego is against Me, I am asking from My servants, if they want My pleasure with themselves, that they must be against their egos."

You may fill whole world with worshipping; it is easy. But to be against your ego once—it is more important. And during this holy month, Allah Almighty is teaching His servants how they can be successful in being against their egos.

Fasting teaches us to be against our egos. Therefore, it is the most important worship that Allah Almighty has ordered for all nations through His prophets. And we must ask forgiveness from Allah Almighty because for so long we have been going along with our egos, not against them, and because for so long they have been going against our Lord and not going with Him. And we are saying, *"Astaghfirullah, astaghfirullah, astaghfirullah..."* [56]

▲

---

[56]"I seek Allah's forgiveness."

12: trusting in allah for our provision

May Allah bless you! Allah Almighty blesses those people who declare war against their egos. Everything, every help, that they may ask, Allah promises to give them, and difficulties are going to be made very easy and unsolved problems are going to be solved by Divine Help.

We must know which things bring Divine Help to ourselves and which things make divine help go away from us. If you know, that is a key, opening to you. Not only from one side will Divine Help come to you; from the Heavens, from the earth, from the East, from the West, from every direction, Divine Help will flow to you, as Allah Almighty is mentioning in the Holy Qur'an, "O people, if you keep your Lord's commands and advice, at each one foot's distance you may eat from the earth and from the Heavens."[57]

If you can keep His Divine Advice to you, He promises to give you everything. Wherever you may step, everything will come to you from the earth, reaching you, or from the Heavens, coming on you. And it is so important a thing; to keep His Divine Advice opens to you everything from every direction. And the contrary, also. It means that if you do not listen to His Divine Advice, from every direction every open door becomes locked.

Therefore, you must be very careful. So many times people are accusing Almighty Allah of not opening the way for them, but that is a meaningless accusation because He gave us one key which opens and another one

---

[57]See, for example, 11:52: "And, O my people, ask forgiveness of your Lord and then turn to Him. He will send [rain from] the sky upon you in abundance and add strength to your strength, so do not turn away as sinners." 71:10-12 is similar.

which locks. We are using the key which locks, not which opens. Through every prophet He has given those keys to His servants. But we are using them in the opposite way, and if you want to open but instead you close or you lock it, it is impossible for it to be opened to you.

Allah Almighty wants a very easy life for His servants; He does not want to make our life a heavy burden on our shoulders. Therefore He guarantees the *rizq*, provision, of His servants by His Divine Promises, saying, "O My servants, don't be worried about your provision. I am that One who is going to give you your provision. You must believe in Me and you must trust in Me. Am I not a Trustworthy One for you?"

What is your answer? We may say "Yes" with our lips but not with our hearts. We are quickly running, quickly working; then how is it true? It can be true only if you believe and trust, saying, "You are the Trustworthy One," and *then* you run. And Allah Almighty never, never forgets you; He does not forget even an ant. And I see that in the morning time, from dawn, birds are flying. They do not plant, they do not grow, they do not do anything but go and come back full.

To us, the children of Adam 🕊, Allah Almighty gives so many promises in His holy books, in the Holy Qur'an, but still we have a doubt. We are not able to say, "O my Lord, You are the Trustworthy One. The Most Trustworthy One is *You*." We aren't able to say that (perhaps we may say it with our lips but not with our hearts). And the most dangerous method that Satan uses to destroy our faith is to make us not believe that Allah Almighty is the Trustworthy One in promising us our provisions, making us to be in doubt: "If I don't work, how can I live? If I haven't any money, how can I live?" A person means to say that with money I may buy provisions, his ego saying to him, "O my good fellow, don't be foolish. Without money you can't live!" That is the advice of our egos to ourselves: "You must have money for living. If not, you can't live."

Once Abu Yazid [al-Bistami], *Sultan al-'Arifin*,[58] was traveling, and he came to a town and entered a big mosque. He prayed behind the *imam*, and then the *imam* turned around, like this, to look at the people, who was coming, who was going.

He saw a strange person; it was clear that he was not from that country. And he asked, "Who are you? From where are you coming? What do you do?"

Bayazid Bistami Hazretleri,[59] may Allah bless him, said, "Nothing!"

"No work?"

"No work!"

"No profession?"

"No profession!"

"Then from where do you eat?"

Then Abu Yazid said, "Let me pray my prayer again. I thought that you were a Muslim but you are not yet Muslim, and I must repeat my prayer. How are you the *imam* here? What are you asking? I thought that you knew that my provision is with my Lord, and yet you are asking, 'From what do you live?'"

And he was saying, "*Subhanallah*, glory to Allah Almighty! You do not trust in Allah Almighty. Why do you not catch cats or dogs and ask them from what they are living?" he asked that *imam*. "You have a dog or a cat? Cats, they have jobs? Dogs—a job, a profession, learned ones? Why are you not asking them but instead catching hold of me to ask me from what I am living? Dogs and cats, from whatever they are living, I am living, also!" he said, very angry.

Particularly in European countries, I don't think that any cat or any dog thinks about its provision. Do you think so? Yes, fat ones here; they

---

[58]The sovereign of the knowers of Allah.

[59]*Hazretleri* (Turkish): his holiness, from the Arabic, *hadrat.*

can carry their owners, even, carrying them away. I don't think that they have any worry within themselves about their provisions. But we human beings, we are not like them.

Its owner is a person and he is trustworthy; his dog or cat never thinks about tomorrow. But *we* are thinking, although the whole world is for ourselves. And Allah Almighty says, "I am your Provider. Do you not believe in Me? Am I not a Trustworthy One for you?" But Satan always comes from that direction, making a doubt in our hearts and beginning to destroy our beliefs.

We must believe that even if Allah Almighty made the whole sky to be covered with iron plates and the whole face of the earth to be rock, so that nothing could fall down from the sky or nothing could come up from that rock—even if they were to be like that, sky and earth, you wouldn't have any right to be in doubt about your provision as long as He says, "I am promising you. I may give *bis-sabab* or *bila sabab*, through means or without means. I am saying that I shall give. To give your your provision, I am not in need of using means."

Once, at the time of Moses 鄒, there was a drought—no water, no rain, and people came to Moses and asked him to go out and make *du'a*, to pray for rain.

And all the people went out. They brought their animals, and then they took away the lambs to one side and the sheep to another side so that the lambs began to cry. And they took the little children, also, with their mothers, so that Allah Almighty might look at them with mercy.

Moses 鄒 took all the Children of Israel and went to a high hill (it was an old custom of prophets to make *du'a* on a place which had no sins on it, clean). They went, and Moses prayed and prayed, but no answer came to his *du'a*. And then he asked, "O my Lord, what is the reason?" because if a prophet asks, rain must come; it *must* rain.

And then Allah Almighty addressed him: "O Moses, among your people there is a *nammam*" (a *nammam* is someone who runs to a husband to talk to him against his wife, or to neighbors, from one door to the next, to make mischief, to give harm—a slanderer). And Allah Almighty was saying that there was one person among that huge crowd, one man who was a slanderer.

Then Moses ﷺ said, "O my Lord, please tell us who that one is so that we may take him away."

"O Moses, I have prohibited people to do that, and now you are asking Me to show you who that one is. But if I were to show you, I would be *nammam* Myself. If I were to say, 'That person,' then I would be *that*."

Then that person, the *nammam*, trembled too much, fearing Allah Almighty and saying within himself, "O my Lord, *tubtu wa raj'atu ilaik*—I repent and I am sorry. O my Lord, forgive me!"

Allah Almighty forgave that person, and then heavy clouds came, and rain. The rains increased, increased, so much that if a person on horseback had gone into the water, it would have covered him. But at the end, no grains. There was nothing in the ears.

And then Moses ﷺ was too angry: "O my Lord, what happened? This has come like bamboo—no grains!"

Then Allah Almighty said, "O Moses, I shall show you My wisdom and My power. Make a fire in a *tannur*!"

A *tannur* is an oven like a big jar, with fire inside. Moses ﷺ made a fire, and then Allah Almighty ordered, "Take a handful of grain and throw it into the fire." And Moses ﷺ did that.

Quickly those grains grew, grew, grew, becoming ears. Although the fire was burning, in the middle of the fire those grains did not burn but quickly became ears. And then Allah Almighty said, "O Moses, I am the powerful One who can do everything. You must believe that I am able to do everything. You asked from Me rain and I sent you rain, as much as you asked for. Ask from Me your provision and I can give. Without rain I can give; even in fire I can give. I am your Lord. *You must believe in your Lord!*"

Yes, we are afraid for tomorrow, but Allah Almighty, the Lord, is saying, "O My servant, I am not asking you today for tomorrow's worshipping. When you come to tomorrow, then I will ask for your prayers for that day. Prayers are at their proper times; before their time I am not asking for them. Then why are you asking today about tomorrow, about next week, next month, next year? *Why are you asking?*"

Therefore, Allah Almighty wants to take more heavy burdens from ourselves so that we may be lighter, we may be more at ease in this life. He wants an easy life for us but we are making it heavier, a heavy burden that we can't carry. If we believe with certainty, then our life is so easy. We have only been ordered to be in the time which we are in; we haven't been ordered to look after one hour later, one day, one week, one month, one year later. That is making troubles and difficulties for the life of mankind.

All creatures have *itmi'nan*, confidence, within themselves. Why not for the children of Adam 🕊, for mankind? What is the reason? No other one among creatures has been given a mind, no, and without minds they are living in confidence, in tranquility. But we have minds and we are not in confidence.

Therefore, we must believe in our Lord, that He is able to do everything, to make everything, to give everything, both what we can imagine or beyond our imagination, also. He is *al-Muqtadir*, All-Powerful to do everything. And at every time Satan works on that point, particularly in our times. In our times he causes too much harm to people, to believers' beliefs, causing the destruction of their beliefs.

In this country there are so many foreigners; I must tell *them*, also. So many millions of foreigners are escaping from their countries and coming to England. I wonder if they are finding another provider in London. Do you think so, or the same One? The same One, the only One—the same One who gives to us here or in our homelands.

We are making our life difficult. That provision was apportioned before the creation of this universe, a long, long time ago, and it is like our shadow, following us, or like our *ajal*, our term of life, following ourselves for the limit of our life.

Our life is within limits, and our provision is within limits, also. You can't escape from death and you can't escape from your provision. You can't eat from *his* provision, he can't eat from *your* provision. Everyone must eat from his own appointed provision and finish and then go. No fear, if you know that. Even if you are in your homeland, those provisions must come to you, because no one else can eat from them. They *must* come to you. ▲

13: making a way to your real personality in the divine presence

By the name of Allah, All-Mighty, All-Merciful, Most Beneficent and Most Munificent. Each time we are saying, "Most Beneficent, Most Munificent." And Allah Almighty is asking His servants to be merciful to His creatures, always mentioning and proclaiming His attributes of mercy.

You must also be merciful to each other because Allah Almighty, with His Mercy Oceans, gives to His creatures, and all creatures in existence take their shares from the Mercy Oceans which belong to His holy Name, *ar-Rahman*. It is impossible to finish those Mercy Oceans which belong to His holy Name, *ar-Rahman*, because everything that belongs to Allah Almighty is endless.

And then, He is also *ar-Rahim*. There are Mercy Oceans which belong to the holy Name *ar-Rahim*, indicating to His servants to be merciful to all other people and to everyone in existence.

We as human beings, the sons of Adam, must be people of much more understanding, as Allah Almighty is teaching us through His prophets and holy books. All of us were in the same universe before coming to this life, everyone's soul coming from the spiritual world or from the Heavens, and it is in *this* form during this life. All of us, we were in the spiritual world, all our souls, but I don't think that we were quarreling or fighting there. Do you think such a thing? Who remembers? Almost no one remembers. We have only certain exceptions, when Allah Almighty opens the veil to His servant. *Then* he knows.

Our Grandshaykh, may Allah bless him, was speaking, and he asked a question: "What is the benefit of all *shari'ats* and *tariqats*? What is the aim of prophets and of their messages? From the beginning up to the end, for what does Allah Almighty send His prophets and His messages, and what is He going to teach people through His *shari'ats*, and through *tariqats*, also?"

Tariqat and *shari'at* are from the same source, no difference, but now people have changed their understanding and are getting a wrong meaning of *tariqat*. *Tariqat* is mysticism in every religion, and it *must* be. As we are not going to be without hearts (you can't be only a form, an external appearance; there is something inside, also), so every religion has some external functions or actions, and some others, also, which are inner, internal. *Must be!* Do you think that oceans or seas are only what we see, blue water, with nothing inside it? So many creatures it covers.

Therefore, you can't find any religion without mysticism; *must be*—yes! And our Grandshaykh was speaking and asking that question: "What is the purpose of every *shari'at* and of *tariqats*? For what are they making people to act, to work, to worship, to fast, to do charities, to believe, or to do anything else?" And he was giving that question's answer: that all the wisdom of *shari'ats* and their orders and actions, in every religion, is because we are, all of us, in prison during this life.

In the womb of your mother you were looking at the Heavens, and also when it comes to this life—for one day, two days, three, four, five, six, seven days mostly—that new baby looks at the Heavens, no veil on its heart's eyes. After that, they are veiled, the veil coming and no more looking. There are only certain exceptions among mankind who are not veiled, ever, not covered. And Grandshaykh said, concerning those exceptions, "I am one of them" (not I, but Grandshaykh was, and when he opened it to me, I was looking; no worry). From the time of his birth up to the end, he was saying, "O Nazim Efendi, I never veiled my heart." And the main purpose and divine wisdoms of *shari'ats* and *tariqats* is only to take away that veil that comes on your heart's eyes; it is only for that opening.

Therefore, the Holy Qur'an begins with the *Surah* of Opening, *al-Fatehah*. That *surah* opens to you. If a person looks at *al-Fatehah* for the meanings which any scholar may know, he may be able to acquire all the meanings of the life of men through those seven verses of the *Surah* of

Opening, and those are the actions of the *Shari'ah* in Islam. But when you keep to that *surah* by the way of *tariqat*, it brings you an opening through your heart.

When you reach that station, when the veils are taken from your heart's eyes, you will find yourself in the same universe that you were in before [in the spiritual world]. We are still there, as the sun is in the sky while it is also on earth; we are saying, "The sun is here," while the sun is in the skies. It is just the same situation for your soul. Everyone's soul is like a shining sun and it has a station in the Heavens, in the Divine Presence, never leaving its worshipping, never leaving its glorifying its Lord, Allah Almighty.

Don't suppose that our souls are sitting in silence, like this. All of them, in the Divine Presence, were glorifying and praising their Lord, Allah Almighty, and they are continuing the same thing. But we are here, and from that shining sun of our soul, only one ray is coming and commanding this body. If the whole of one soul's power were to appear in this world, it would quickly melt, going away; it would not be able to carry it. Therefore Allah Almighty only sends one ray representing your personality, which is in the Divine Presence, to come into this world.

And we are trying to be in contact with our realities, with our real existence in the Heavens and in the Divine Presence. Therefore, prophets, messengers, came from Allah Almighty to make a connection through our hearts to those heavenly stations.

That is the meaning of all the practices in every religion, and finally, the aim of every practice or worship in Islam is to make a connection from yourself to your real personality in the Divine Presence. The one who may reach his divine position is a real deputy of his Lord, Allah Almighty. That is the meaning of the Prophet's saying, "*Mutu qabla an tamutu*—die before you die," so that you may reach real life in the Divine Presence.

Whoever "dies before dying" reaches peace, absolute peace and absolute happiness; he reaches his universe that Allah Almighty gives to him and makes him *sultan*, sovereign, in his territory in the Divine Presence. They do not sit like this, all together, but in an endless divine territory, each one taking what Allah Almighty gives to him, and no one knows his *muhimmah*, importance, in the Divine Presence.

Therefore, as much as you improve in divine knowledge, which passes through yourself, self-knowledge, you may feel more refreshment in your heart. You may feel that you are in an endless world, never inside a narrow space, and as much as you improve in divine knowledge, you will want more because you will receive more pleasure and ask for more. Perhaps you may send a little boy to school by force because he has not yet tasted anything of knowledge, but when he reaches a position of tasting what he reads and understanding it, he is going to be pleased with learning and to ask for more and more.

As much as you may have of divine knowledge, it will give you more pleasure, more happiness, more satisfaction, and we are also in need to know or to ask for more divine knowledge in order to reach peace during our lives. And the way to divine knowledge passes through ourselves. When you are sitting in your station in the Divine Presence—I mean to say, when there is a connection from your heart to your real personality in the Divine Presence—there will always flow from it to you, to your heart, more divine knowledge through yourself, because divine knowledge comes to your real personality in the Divine Presence, and you may take from there to your heart, and your pleasure will grow, never ending. Therefore, we must try to practice the spiritual ways of Islam because it is important and necessary for our lives in order to reach real life and to reach real deputies' stations while we are in this life.

Three times each day Allah Almighty gives His servants more favors. You must be *musta'id*, ready, to receive more divine favors. Those who find their Lord's divine favors find them during these three times.

During the twenty-four hours, from *'Asr* up to *Maghrib*[60] is one of the most precious times when the divine manifestations come on people, and you must be ready to receive that with your heart. Then, from *Maghrib* up

---

[60]That is, between the time of *'Asr*, the late afternoon prayer, up to *Maghrib*, sunset, when the fourth prayer of the day is observed

to 'Isha.[61] And when night passes and there remains the last one-third of the night, that is the most precious time; the one who wants spiritual improvement, he must look after that time. Those first two times are also such precious times, but the most precious of all is during the third and last part of the night before dawn; it may be three hours, may be four hours or five hours or more, according to the length of the night. You must be ready at that time to accept the spiritual and heavenly rays that touch your heart.

No one reaches his Divine station without awakening at least as long as the time of praying two *rak'ats* before dawn every night. That is a limited time, but at least you must be there, ready, even if only for two *rak'ats*. You may take a shower, *ghusl*—that is best; either a shower or *wudu*—and then stand facing *qiblah,* pray two *rak'ats* and then sit, seeing to it that no one is with you except One, not your wife or your or your parents or your friends. No one may be with you .

Only One is going to be with you, and you must think that at this time I am here alone; everyone has gone from me and only One is with me. My Lord is with me! From every direction, inside, outside, He is with me, and, O my Lord, *I am with You!* Then there rains upon you from the Heavens rays of lights, Divine lights, preparing your heart, taking it away from this life's preoccupations and making you in the Divine Presence.

One, two, three, four, five nights; ten nights, twelve, twenty, thirty nights; if you are keeping that with your Lord, then it should be yours. He should grant to you some lights in your heart, and it is the beginning of an opening for you. And then, when you feel that opening, you must continue, because the most important miracle is to continue on your way without turning back. And every forty nights a new light comes to gather in your heart until that light cuts the veil in your heart, making an operation, taking it away, and you are looking at your universe that Allah Almighty granted to you. ▲

---

[61]From sunset up to the time of total darkness, when 'Isha, the fifth prayer of the day, is observed.

14: restraining our egos from their desires

'Innama yuwaffa-s-sabiruna ajruhum bi-ghairi hisab'[62]—we are in need of patience, everyone. Yes; the most important thing is to be patient during this life. Allah Almighty gives to *shakirin*, the people who are thankful for His favors, numbered rewards. But for *sabirin*, people who can be patient, the angels put down their pens. They are unable to write the amount of reward, and Allah Almighty Himself writes and gives rewards for those people who are patient.

Now, there are three kinds of patience. First, this world is not a place for being in pleasure always; so many times it is a very heavy burden, this life, and you must be patient. There may be illness; every kind of trouble may come on people. It is outside our wills. We are not able to take it away; by itself it comes on us. Therefore you must be patient, because everything in this life is within limits, and even if you are not patient, that trouble will never go away till its time is finished. Nothing continues; there must be a limit—for pleasure or for sadness, for troubles, for every kind of a thing. And Allah Almighty gives rewards to those who are patient.

And second, we must be patient for worshipping. To make *wudu*, to do *ghusl*, washing; to do prayers; for fasting or for pilgrimage—for all of them we are in need to be patient because without patience you can't do them. Your *nafs* never likes them, and you are forcing yourself to pray, to make *wudu*, to get up for night prayers, to do mid-day prayers; and for fasting and for *Hajj*, pilgrimage, we are also in need to be patient because our

---

[62]"Indeed, the patient will be given their reward without reckoning." (39:10)

nafs, our ego, never likes them. More than for the first one, Allah Almighty rewards His servants because they are praying and worshipping.

And the third thing that is important for being patient is that you must keep your ego from prohibited actions because your ego rushes at them. Most important of the three is to be patient when your *nafs* or ego rushes toward its desires, and you put on reins and control it. *"Inna-n-nafsa la-ammaratun bis-sou"*[63]—no doubt that our ego always orders us the worst things, not only ordering bad but worse and worst, and if you do not keep its orders, it gets to be very angry with you. Therefore, most people are afraid of their ego, of their *nafs*; so that it should not be angry with them, they look after their *nafs* very well, excellently. And the Prophet 🕮 said, "O my Companions, do you know someone who, if you respect him and give him everything, in the face of your favors and respects to him he puts you down, and, on the contrary, if you put him down, he gives you too much respect?"

The Companions were very surprised, asking, "What kind of a fellow is that? We respect him and he puts us down, but if we put him down then he gives too much respect to us—what kind of a fellow or friend is that?"

And the Prophet 🕮 answered, saying, "That is your *nafs*, your ego." The more you give it respect, the more it puts you down, and the more you are able to be strict with it, the more it respectful to you, saying, "O my lord, as you like!" As long as you say to it, "O my lord, as you like!" it puts *you* down.

We are respecting our egos too much and saying, "As you like!" and we are working for their refreshment and happiness and pleasure. If for one day we would do for our Lord as we are doing for our *nafs*, we would be able to fly without wings; we would be able to blink our eyes and then open them in Mecca, or, like this, open them in America. But the whole day, the whole night, we are only thinking about how we can make our ego pleased, how we can give pleasure to our *nafs*. Is it not true? Who says that it is not like this?

---

[63]"Indeed, the *nafs* [lower self, ego] is a persistent enjoiner of evil." (12:53)

You must not give that chance to your *nafs*. But we *do* give it; therefore we are in need to be patient when our *nafs* rushes toward its desires. It is impossible to keep yourself if you do not think of your Lord's pleasure. *Nafs* is the one which is against its Lord, and if it is against your Lord, how can it be with *you*? And it is the most difficult patience that we can practice, to stop our *nafs'* desires.

We have, in every religion and particularly in Islam, methods by which we may be able to keep our egos from their desires and to make them under our control, but it needs patience. We are taking some power, a little bit, from fasting, but it is not enough during Ramadan only. After Ramadan, also, we must practice keeping our *nafs* far away from its desires.

On some days, for controlling our *nafs*, our ego, we may fast, but not fasting from eating and drinking. You may fast with your eyes; some days you may fast with your tongue; some days you may fast with your hands; some days you may fast with your feet. If you can't do it the whole day, you may do it for some hours, even for one hour; you may say, "For one hour I am going to fast with my eyes, with my tongue, with my hands, with my feet." And most important, also, is to be able to fast through your thoughts, not allowing any false thoughts to come to your heart. Every *tariqat*, all forty-one *tariqats*, are teaching their followers to finally make a control on their hearts through their thoughts. If your heart is not clean from bad thoughts, it is impossible for the power and lights of real faith to enter into your heart.

You must know how your heart is going to be clean. If at any time a bad or false thought comes into your heart, it means that you are not guarding the doors of your heart, you are not controlling it. Satan is always looking around to find a way to enter your heart. When he enters, he puts bad thoughts into your heart, and those bad thoughts become bad intentions and bad intentions go through your veins.

When they go through your veins, then your eyes start to look and your hands want to touch and your feet want to run after prohibited things. Therefore, it is impossible for someone to claim that his heart is all right. If he does, I am asking, "You never think bad thoughts? They never come to your heart when you go outside, when you are not in the mosque?" Out-side—yes! If he is able to say "No," then I am asking, "You are telling the truth, or lying?" And Allah knows who is true and who is a liar; and who-ever tells a lie, *"La'natu-Llahi 'ala-l-kadhibin,"*[64] Allah curses liars.

Once a grandshaykh, 'Abdul-Khaliq al-Ghujdavani, may Allah bless him, ordered a *murid* of his to keep his thoughts under control. If anything came to his heart of this world, this life's pleasures, he was to make *ghusl*, complete washing. And that grandshaykh also said the same about thoughts concerning *Akhirah*, the Hereafter. He meant to say that if a per-son thinks about rewards for his worshipping, such as, "I am fasting and I am expecting rewards from Allah Almighty because I fasted," or, "I am praying and I am expecting the rewards of Paradise because I am worship-ping," that thought is falsehood.

You must not expect a reward from Allah Almighty for your worship-ping because, firstly, it is not suitable to be presented in the Divine Pres-ence, our worshipping. You must not look at it as something good to pre-sent to Allah Almighty's Divine Presence; rather, you must be ashamed.

What are we doing? As He ordered us, we are praying. Then what is the reason that the Prophet advised to make *istighfar*, to ask forgiveness, after praying, ordering that, when you finish *salat*, prayers, you must say, *"Astaghfirullah, astaghfirullah, ya Rabbana. Ya Rabbi, 'ghfir wa-'rham, wa Anta Khairu-l-Rahimin"?*[65] Because you must be ashamed of that prayer; it is not suitable to be presented to Allah Almighty. Then how can you say that you are proud of your worshipping or your praying—and ask for a reward, also? Instead, you must be ashamed; you must say, "O my Lord, it is not suitable for You."

Once a good-hearted person came to pray. After all the others had come to the *masjid*, he was the last one, coming and praying at the door. He

[64] (3:61)

[65]"I seek Your forgiveness, I seek Your forgiveness, O our Lord. O my Lord, forgive and have mercy, and You are the best of the merciful.

was afraid and said to himself, "If people look at me, they may beat me and throw me out as a person not necessary to come to this *masjid*, saying, 'Go away!'" He saw himself as the last one, as the dirtiest one, as the most false one, so that he was the last to enter the *jama'at*[66] and the first one to quickly run away.

That is a very good characteristic, humbleness, and it is correct. Everyone must look at himself in such a way in order to be humble. If Allah Almighty did not cover our bad actions, it would be difficult for anyone to walk in the streets, but Allah Almighty covers with His mercy our *'uyub*, bad deeds. And in the orders of *tariqats*, if anyone asks a reward for his praying and worshipping, that is a bad thought. He must take it away and renew his *wudu* because of that bad thought.

We are praying and fasting only because He ordered it and because He is that One whom we must worship or who is to be worshipped—*that One!* As Rabi'at al-Adawiyah,[67] may Allah bless her, said, "O my Lord, I am not praying to you for the sake of Paradise and I am not praying to You for the fear of Your Fire. But You are that One who must be praised, must be worshipped; You are the Lord. Even if You had not ordered it, still we would have to worship You because You are that One who *must* be worshipped and praised and glorified."

Then that *murid* of Ghudjdavani, may Allah bless him and forgive that *murid* and ourselves with him—so many thoughts came to that *murid* one after the other, one after the other, thoughts about *dunya*, about this life, and he had been ordered to make a new *ghusl* each time. That day he couldn't find time to pray five times because of *ghusl*, washing.

That is an important practice to take away bad thoughts. They do not go quickly; Satan does not go quickly or easily—never! You stop him from this side and then he comes from that side, saying, "Come with me, come

---

[66]Congregation.

[67]The well-known saint, Rabi'ah Basri.

with me! With *me* you can find pleasure." And our ego says that, also. Our ego is too much pleased with him, running after him.

Allah gives us a chance every Ramadan but we are losing it *after* Ramadan. Up to the end, we are trying to make a control, but each day we are only guarding our stomachs. And our thoughts—thoughts are more difficult; we are not even guarding our eyes, our tongues, our feet. Thoughts are more important than that, because thoughts are thrown into your heart; if you do not control your heart, thoughts are thrown into it.

There is a kind of fly which goes on meat, a black fly. (Your country is too improved; you don't see it here, but in our country we have too many. If you need some, we may send them to you for exhibiting. You can make money, too much money, if exhibiting!) That kind of a fly goes on flesh in the butchery, quickly putting its eggs there, and quickly they grow. After a week with no frigidaire, they multiply too much—*multimillionaire*! That opens the way.

Like this, if a person is heedless of his heart, quickly Satan puts eggs there. While you are turning from this side to that side, those eggs, bad thoughts' eggs, open and become intentions. Thoughts are thrown into your heart like the eggs of Satan. Then satanic intentions open, and if you do not control your thoughts first, for intentions it is impossible. You *must* run after them—by looking, by speaking, by running; yes. That is terrible! Intention is in connection with thoughts. Therefore, you must be very careful of your heart, controlling it.

In airports there is strict control of people so that useless people do not come into the country, making it bad. Yes, the English government keeps security, saying, "This person is no good; we don't accept him." But our hearts are open; everything comes and goes—doesn't matter, like a pub! In a pub, is any person forbidden? Everyone goes, comes, goes, comes, putting money, drinking, going. *And on your heart, no control?* If there is no control on your heart, Satan throws in false thoughts and bad intentions, and then endless troubles and problems come, and you say, "How can we solve it?"

No solution! If we do not look after our hearts, this world's, this life's, complexities are never going to be solved; no solution! You must clean yourself from bad thoughts, you must look after your heart. People always are looking outward; even Muslim people, the Muslim world, also, have been cheated by external things. They are neglecting their hearts, saying, "No function for the heart. Islam is only outward things—*taharah*,[68] *wudu*, *ghusl*, praying," and praying for half-an-hour like this, half-an-hour like this, half-an-hour like this.

That is not praying. You must pray with your heart. It is not to show that you are so long in praying; instead, you must pray with your *heart*. Allah Almighty looks at your heart and says, "My servant is praying now, but his heart is with whom?" And when your heart is with your Lord Almighty in *salat*, that is real prayer.

Once a scholar came to a shaykh; he had heard that he was a great grandshaykh and came to visit him. When he arrived, that shaykh was the *imam* in the *Maghrib* prayer. And the scholar, that *'alim*, prayed behind him and he heard him reciting incorrectly, with too many mistakes. Then he said to himself, "Oh, I must pray alone. It is no good to pray with that person."

He prayed, and then he was in need of going out to repeat his *wudu*. When he went out, suddenly a lion rushed out, attacking him, and he ran— *oh-h-h!!!* And the shaykh was looking. "Go! I am saying that you must not disturb my guest. Go away!" the shaykh said, and the big lion ran away.

That *'alim* was very surprised, saying, "O my Lord, how can it be?"

"O my brother," the grandshaykh said, "you are trying to make your outward appearance perfect, ornamented. Therefore you are afraid of the lion. But we are trying to make our hearts perfect with our Lord, and that lion is afraid of ourselves."

---

[68]Cleanliness and purification.

You understand? May Allah forgive us! We are in need to listen too much so that perhaps some good thoughts may be in our hearts, opening during this holy month. That is our hope from our Lord, Allah Almighty.

▲

15: keeping firm our steps toward our lord

Who is a prophet? Prophets must be well-known because we are living in a time when people are fighting against prophets and going with devils. And from the beginning, devils have been coming to people to cheat them and deceive them, beginning by deceiving Adam ﷺ, the first man, who was created in Paradise. Allah Almighty gave him the honor of being His deputy, but then jealousy and envy made everything worse and then worst.

If a person is not a sincere servant to his Lord, envy destroys his faith, and it destroys every good action of people. The worst and most dangerous and terrible bad characteristic is envy; you can't find anything worse than envy. And envy is in hearts; its *maqar*, abode, is the heart. Where envy is settled in a heart, it burns every good deed that we do.

Satan was a worshipper. He did not leave even one square foot on the earth or in the Heavens without putting his forehead on it in *sajdah*, prostration, to his Lord, Allah Almighty. And Allah Almighty also gave him from knowledge; as much as he asked He gave, and Allah Almighty made him, also, a teacher for the angels. He had a special station, a high station, among creatures; everything was excellent. But, as our Grandshaykh was always saying, if anyone wants a reward in return for his actions, his worshipping, that person is on the same level as the one who goes and worships the Cross, no difference. It is so terrible, because Allah Almighty is asking, "*Ala lil-Lahi-d-dinu-l-khalis?*"[69] asking worshipping to be for the sake of His Divine Face only.

---

[69]"Unquestionably, the pure religion is for Allah." (39:3)

If He did not promise His servants to give them Paradise for their worshipping or if He did not threaten them with Hell, it would be enough of a favor for us, as His servants whom He brought from nothingness into existence, to give our glorifying and praise, our endless thanks, to Him, even if there was nothing else. And, O believers, everything in existence is glorifying its Lord and saying *"Subhanallah!"*—glorifying Him with so many kinds of *tasbih*, glorification. Even ants or creatures that are less than ants are saying it and glorifying their Lord.

For what? *Because He created them and is looking after them, creating and giving them a position in existence.* That is an ant, that is another insect among millions of kinds of insects or other creatures, but we are saying that even the smallest one is so happy because it is an honor to come into existence. And what is that honor? *Because the Creator created them, giving them a personality in existence. They are something in existence and they are glorifying their Lord.*

But what about you, O children of Adam, when the whole universe was created for you? Allah Almighty just created it for the honor of His deputy, and you are that deputy, you are candidates to be deputies. If you walk on the same steps as those who reached the real stations of deputies, you will arrive, you *must* reach, also.

But we are not walking on that path. We are in need of *qadam as-sidq*. What is that? *Qadam as-sidq* means true steps, not *"Thumma amanu, thumma kafaru; thumma amanu, thumma kafaru."*[70] As Allah Almighty is saying, "Sometimes, O people, O servants, you are coming to Me, worshipping Me, glorifying Me, but sometimes I see you running after Iblis, after Satan, after devils. You are respecting and listening to and working for devils! What is this? Your steps are not correct!"

Qadam as-sidq is that, if you put your foot on the right path, with the right step, you must be firm, not taking it back. But we are living in a time when it is so difficult. If anyone intends or puts his foot on the right path, one thousand devils rush on him, attacking him and trying to take that foot

---

[70]"Then they believed *(amanu)*, then disbelieved *(kafaru)*; then believed, then disbelieved," a paraphrase of 4:137.

back from that right step, some of them crying, some of them saying, "Ohh! You must not do this because we are too young. We are still young people, we must live some of our lives!" Yes, for ladies, for young men— aren't they crying to you? Yes, crying and saying, "It is not the time to be on truth or on the true way, not time yet. We are young! When you are going to be like that shaykh, it won't matter."

Yes, they are saying this, too many advisors, devils, giving advice. Not millions—*billions* of advisors you may find for yourself: "Don't put this foot there; take it back. You must live!" Therefore, the most miraculous thing for a servant is to continue, because it is not easy to put your foot on the right path, on the true way, and to continue because you must move it forward for taking the next step, and one thousand devils are all catching at you. You must be strong enough, powerful enough, to carry all of them, to move to the second and third and fourth step. When it is *"Thumma amanu, thumma amanu, thumma amanu,"*[71] you must reach, but when you listen to those devils and their armies, then you must take your foot back— *"Thumma amanu, thumma kafaru."* The Prophet ﷺ says that Paradise is going to be so close to a person that after just one step he may be in Paradise, but then he takes back his steps and goes to the way of Hells.

Therefore, it is so difficult to be firm on the right steps, and Allah Almighty is asking the right steps from you, not with Him here [in the mosque] but outside with devils, with Satan. Therefore, if a person may worship as if with the worshipping of all people, it is not important. Important is to fix your feet or your steps on the true way—on truth, toward Allah. Don't turn your face away from *qiblah*.

You are putting this face toward *qiblah*, but what about your heart—to where is your heart looking? You must know; you must control your heart, the direction of your heart's face. That is the meaning of *"Ala lil-Lahi-d-dinu-l-khalis?"*

You are saying, *"Mustaqbila-l-qiblah*—O our Lord, we are turning our face toward *qiblah*," but what about your *heart*? *Qiblah* is the Ka'bah but

---

[71] "Then they believed, then they believed, then they believed."

where is your heart? Your face is toward that Ka'bah and the Ka'bah is the House of the Lord. You are entering it but not looking for the Lord?

Therefore, it is a difficult time, or the most difficult time, that we are living in in our days. One century or fifty or sixty years ago you could find most people asking for faith, for religions, for the ways of the prophets, but now you can't find people to help you on the ways of the prophets. Most people are becoming advertisers for devils, cheating each other, deceiving each other, saying, "Come, leave that! It is superstition." Super *foolish* people, and making the prophets to be of no value in our time but making devils too important!

The Seal of the Prophets, Sayyidina Muhammad ﷺ, told about this, and, just as he said, it is appearing. What is prophethood and who is a prophet? The one who informs people about the future, about what will come on them, that is a prophet, because no one can know by ordinary means what is coming tomorrow or after tomorrow—even after one hour, let alone the future. Who can know what is coming after centuries or after thousands of years? Only prophets, and those are miracles for the prophets—to tell about something which will come after centuries. And as much as all the other prophets informed people about the last days and about the Last Day, and what are the signs and what will come on people, the Seal of the Prophets, Sayyidina Muhammad ﷺ, informed us most about what is going to happen day by day, and it is correct. If you look at his life and at his sayings, you can find everything among his *hadith*, his holy sayings, that is now appearing.

And we are saying now, today, that he informed and warned his nation, his *ummah*, about *dajjals*, anti-Christs—so many. Dajjal,[72] the Anti-Christ, is the one who is well-known, but the Prophet ﷺ said that thirty anti-Christs would come, but not "king-sized" ones. The king-sized one is one, so big, but thirty little ones will come to make people ready or to prepare them for his acceptance, for his reception. And thirty dirty *dajjals* have already been among people on earth, living or passed away; you can see. I

---

[72]The Arch-Deceiver or False Messiah who will appear at the end-time, prior to the return of Jesus Christ ﷺ to this world, as mentioned in numerous *hadiths*.

am not saying their dirty names—it is not an honor—but everyone knows who they are, these dirty persons who are calling people to deny the existence of the Lord, Almighty Allah.

They are speaking in the name of 'knowledge,' but they are liars and they are deputies for the big Dajjal. Now, throughout East and West, and even in the Muslim world, they are working. Their bad ideas are planted among the hearts of Muslim people as well; there are so many followers for them there, also. Therefore, it is a terrible time. *Tuba*, good tidings and honor and happiness for the one who can put his feet in the footsteps of the Holy Prophet, beloved Muhammad ﷺ.

You must be very careful, because their followers are not millions but billions on earth. Therefore there is coming a penalty from Allah Almighty—the greatest war, which will take away six out of every seven. During the world wars only millions were going, but now, because most people are followers, millions following the ways of the Dajjal, the Anti-Christ, therefore that event is coming, and out of seven, six will pass on.

Don't be sorry about what is happening on earth; all *awliya* are saying this. Don't be sorry, even if they are from your friends, from your family. Allah Almighty will ask them, "Wasn't there anything that proved My existence? Didn't you ever see anything that might be a proof or might be a witness for My existence in the universe? What was in your head—straw or a brain? *What was in your head?* How *could* you say that no Lord is in existence?" Yes. Therefore, don't be sorry that those who are denying the existence of Allah Almighty should be under that difficult penalty which is coming.

You must look after yourself, and Allah Almighty likes your steps to be toward Him. As your face is turned to *qiblah*, your heart must be turned to Allah, not to *dunya*, to this world. Allah Almighty created this world without looking, and *dunya* is the enemy of Allah because it takes people to itself, taking people's hearts to itself, taking the love of people to itself, not letting people's love to be for their Lord.

Therefore *dunya* is the enemy of Allah, the enemy of prophets, the enemy of *mumins*, believers, and the enemy of all people. Yes, if Allah Almighty had been looking when He created it, it would have been Paradise. But it is not Paradise. People are quarreling, fighting, saying, "This is for me," and you are saying, "It is not, it is for me!" while it is not for me or for you but it is for Him only, under His command. And you are coming as customers come to a hotel and fight: "This is for me! This belongs to me!" *Yahu, not* for you! There is an Owner, a Proprietor—yes? And people are claiming that they are such clever ones, but still they are fighting for this world, for this life.

Therefore, O believers, Allah Almighty gives to everyone a throne, a throne in his heart, and says, "Let Me be there! Don't let anyone else come in; only let *Me* be there. For that throne which is in your heart, don't let anyone else come there." And we are opening it—a free country, free territory, everyone going, coming. I have a key which I brought from Cyprus in my pocket because I closed my house so that no one may enter it except me. Yes; you, also? But for our heart, we are not thinking to make it under control. We are leaving it; anyone may come and go, free house.

Yes, you must think about it. This life is not really a life. We are created for real life, and real life cannot be reached until you give your heart to its Owner and put its Owner there. Otherwise, you may be with the Anti-Christ and his followers. Everyone has been given enough mind to understand, and Allah Almighty is asking from ourselves at least the minimum of understanding. If we don't have that, we are not *mukallaf*, responsible. If we can't understand, no responsibility, but I think that Allah Almighty gives everyone enough mind for understanding about this life and the Creator.

May Allah Almighty forgive us. We are in need to ask forgiveness from Allah Almighty, and the Prophet 鸞, said, "O my nation, I am asking forgiveness from my Lord seventy times every day."

If he asked seventy times, seventy million is too little for ourselves. We *must* ask forgiveness. Asking forgiveness, *istighfar*, makes our wrong steps to be correct steps and turns our hearts toward His Divine Face. And we are asking and saying, *"Astaghfirullah . . ."* ▲

16: the importance of wisdoms

People are coming into Islam, *alhamdulillah*.[73] That is a good tidings, good news, for believers. And most are coming into Islam in Western countries. *Alhamdulillah*, it is a proof that the active power of Islam is like the day it came.

Here there are so many brothers and sisters, and all of them except me are young people; I am not seeing any old ones. All of you are young, *subhanallahi-l-'Aliyyi-l-'Adhim!*[74] If Islam acts on young people it is right. It is perfect, also, because you can run out, and this is London; everything that your egos are asking for you can easily find. Which thing is keeping you here? That is a spiritual power that affects your hearts and that is going to be so victorious on devils and evils.

Now, there is an important question about something which is a problem for new Muslims coming into Islam in Western countries: What they should do for learning and practicing Islam?

Now in our time, a lot of people are coming to Western countries to call people into Islam, but as I see, they are the most fanatical people in their countries, and they are also such hard people. Islam is the most tolerant religion that Allah Almighty has sent to His servants, but they never understand about tolerance in Islam. They want Muslims to be as they were in the time of the Prophet ﷺ, saying that anyone who believes and accepts Islam must keep all the rules in Islam.

---

[73]Praise be to Allah.
[74]Glory be to Allah, the Most High, the Almighty.

That is perfection, but they are not considering that all the rules in Islam did not come at once, on the first day. Allah Almighty could have sent all the rules and all the Qur'an in one day, in one hour; the angel Gabriel could have brought it all, saying, "This is your Book." But Allah Almighty did not do that. Instead, He sent all the rules of Islam over a period of twenty-three years. Is it not true? In twenty-three years the rules of Islam came to be complete.

We are not saying that the rules of Islam are not to be with people in our time. We believe that all its rules are suitable for the nature of man, but we are not prepared for those rules at once. When we make *Shahadah*, saying, "We bear witness to the unity and existence of God, and the prophethood and the Message of Prophet Muhammad ﷺ," saying that we are witnesses to it, that we accept it, it doesn't mean that we are ready to carry all the rules of Islam at that moment. If you say that it does, it means that you do not understand any of the wisdoms for the coming of the Holy Qur'an over twenty-three years; so if you say this, you must make an operation on the heads of people, to cut them open and bring the Book, putting it inside. Otherwise it is impossible.

Therefore, when the Prophet ﷺ informed us about the signs of the last days, he said that when the Last Day approaches, there would be in Islam people without wisdom, and wisdoms are more precious than knowledge. Allah Almighty says, "*Wa man yu'ta-l-hikmata fa-qad utia khairan kathira,*[75] the one who has been given wisdoms has been given all treasures." Therefore, a little bit of wisdom is more precious than all knowledge without wisdoms, as a diamond is more precious than a great amount of coal.

In our time we have knowledge. But we are not in need of knowledge; instead, we are in need of wisdoms. We have thousands, perhaps hundreds of thousands of scholars, but they have only knowledge, without wisdoms.

They may be unhappy with my words, but I must say them. We are in need of wisdoms, and Allah Almighty says that wisdoms are not given to everyone. Wisdoms do not come from outside; the sources of wisdoms

---

[75] 2:269.

come through hearts. You get wisdoms by reading books? No; it is something that you have been given through your heart. Therefore the Prophet ﷺ says, *"Man akhlasa arba'ina sabaha, la-fajarat yanabi'-l-hikmah min qalbihi 'ala lisanihi."*[76] He is saying that if anyone can be a sincere worshipper for forty days—and *ikhlas*, sincerity, means never letting anything of his ego's desires be involved or interfere with his worship for forty days—then Allah Almighty opens in his heart the sources of wisdoms.

But it is not easy. We are following the way of the mind, and that means that we are never given any wisdoms. Yes, the most knowledge that anyone had been given was given to Satan. No one among all scholars could compete with Satan; he would be victorious. But nothing of wisdoms does he have.

If he had only minimum wisdom, he would have been the first to make *sajdah*, prostration, to Adam, respecting his Lord's command. Before anyone else, he would have made *sajdah* when Allah Almighty ordered the angels to make *sajdah* to Adam. But he hasn't any wisdom. Therefore he fell and was thrown out.

Therefore, we are not in need of knowledge. But I am seeing that each one of the new Muslim people, here or in America or England or France or Germany, quickly wants to learn Arabic—to go to Egypt, to go to Azhar,[77] to go to Hijaz; even to Pakistan, also, they are going to learn. They want to learn Arabic or to learn Qur'an, to learn *Hadith*, to be scholars.

Yes, we know that there is a *hadith* from the Prophet ﷺ, saying; *"Talaba-l-'ilma faridatun 'ala kulli muslim wa muslimah"*—Allah Almighty makes it obligatory on every believer, man or woman, to acquire knowledge, *'ilm*. But what are its limits? Because for everything there is a secret desire, *shahwata-l-khafiyah*. For everyone, there are secret desires of their egos which make people to be on false ways, to think that Islam is only something to

---

[76]"Whoever is sincere [to his Lord] for forty days, springs of wisdom will flow forth from his heart upon his tongue."

[77]The world-famous university in Cairo.

know, and a person begins on the way of seeking knowledge—more, more, more, more, more, more knowledge, running, running, running, and it is impossible to find an end for knowledge—and he gets to be tired and finally becomes forgetful, also, because of so much taking. Then he can't carry it and begins to fall down until, at the end, if he can keep even *Kalimata-sh-Shahadah*,[78] it is all right. Yes; I am seeing our Western Muslim brothers and sisters. They are mostly interested in learning, learning, learning and knowing, and without knowing where they should stop.

Imam 'Adham, the Greatest *Imam*, Abu Hanifah, whose *madhhab*,[79] way, millions of people are following, was explaining the meaning of that *hadith* that makes it obligatory on believers to learn or to know.[80] And he was saying, "*Afdala-l-'ilm*, the most precious knowledge that you can have, is only that which is regarding or which concerns yourself," or, as we may say, about what is for you and what is against you: to know everything that may be for you, giving you benefit here and Hereafter, and which thing harms you or gives you trouble here and punishment here and Hereafter.

Only *that* is important to know. It doesn't mean that you are going to learn all the Holy Qur'an and all the *hadiths* of the Prophet 鐃, and all books that are written or every kind of knowledge that Islam brought; it doesn't have such a meaning. But Western people have a deep desire to read, to learn, and they are not changing this characteristic of theirs. Therefore, when they become Muslims, like our brother here—he is asking for a teacher to teach him Arabic and then the meanings of the Holy Qur'an, the meanings of *hadith*, and it is going to be a heavy burden on him. And I am saying to him, "Stop! No need. Only what you may meet with during your life you must learn and you must practice."

That is important: to know or to learn in order to practice, not simply to know, to possess knowledge; no. We are in need of more knowledge only to practice it and to use it in our fight with our egos. You acquire

---

[78]The Declaration of Faith, the utterance through which one enters Islam.

[79]School of Islamic jurisprudence *(fiqh)*.

[80]Referring to *"Talaba-l-'ilma faridatun 'ala kulli muslim wa muslimah,"* cited in the preceding paragraph.

knowledge in order to reach wisdoms because without wisdoms it is impossible to stop your ego's attacking and fighting you.

Wisdoms are like atomic bombs on your ego but other knowledges are only simple weapons, and in our time they are not going to work. Simple weapons are nothing now. As the last days approach, the weapons of devils, the weapons of Satan, are improving, also, to take people away from faith and beliefs. But as Satan is improving in his attacks and the methods that he uses to make people without belief and without faith, so *awliya* are using wisdoms to defeat Satan and his assistants and helpers.

Therefore, this is from those tricks, satanic tricks. If Satan is not able to prevent someone from coming into Islam or from believing, then he uses another method, to make him be tired. When a person is tired, finished; no more can he follow the way or the rules of Islam. And Satan uses his new methods on new believers, saying, "Oh, now you are Muslim, you must keep *all* the rules. Otherwise it is impossible; you are not Muslim!"

Five times a day prayer? One time is enough for you as a new Muslim, and Allah Almighty accepts even only one *sajdah* a day. So many Muslims are not making even that one *sajdah*, although they are Muslims. They are not saying that we are *kafir*, unbeliever; no, they are Muslims. I can show you here in London Turks who are Muslims; they are not making even one *sajdah* each day. Then why are you saying "Five times" for new Muslims? Five times worshipping is perfection. You may say, "It is enough for you to make one *sajdah* daily."

Before, he wasn't doing *anything* but now you are saying, "No. You must learn the Holy Qur'an, all of it, and you must pray five times, and you must fast all of Ramadan, and you must be ready to go to *Hajj*." That is completion, that is the height, but he must reach that completion step by step. But quickly Satan comes, saying, "No—you are not Muslim if you don't do it all," and Satan has representatives, also, among people, to bring down their beliefs or to destroy them.

Therefore, Allah Almighty, in His divine wisdom, at first ordered the *sahabah* to pray only two *rak'ats* in the morning, and then came two *rak'ats* also at *Maghrib*, sunset time. Then, years later, came the order for five times.

We may use the same way, using wisdoms, and we may say to people, "If the *sahabah*, the Companions of Muhammad ﷺ, could pray only two *rak'ats* in the beginning, what is wrong if we say for new Muslims, 'Make one *sajdah* each day—enough'?" We are using this wisdom in this way, and then, when I come the following year, I see those people praying all the prayers. I didn't say to them to pray five times but they are saying, "We can do it now." I advised them only to pray two *rak'ats*, but they are happy now with five times; they are asking for more.

Therefore, we are in need of wisdoms, and wisdoms come through your heart. And you may keep forty days. I am not saying to keep forty days and each day for twenty-four hours to be occupied with worship, no, but I may say to you, Only once a day you may do a worship, at midnight or before *Fajr* time, before dawn, so that no one is with you except your Lord. If you can't take a shower, *ghusl*, you may do *wudu*. Then you may pray two *rak'ats* standing facing *qiblah* and say, "No one is in existence except You, and I am nothing. And I am with You and You are with me"; nothing to say.

Do it, repeat it, for forty nights. Then wisdoms will open a little bit in your heart. Through wisdom comes a light which makes clear this darkness in your world, and you may find a way to go on.

That is for forty days, the easiest method. It may be for five minutes; enough for you, but if you continue with that for forty days, you should find a big benefit. You should find yourself closer to your Lord, and that is important—to feel that you are closer to your Lord. ▲

17: advice for new muslims

Islam as a religion has rules from Allah Almighty, and Islam teaches people what are the perfect conditions for them during this life and hereafter. And in Islam Allah Almighty does not force people; He only asks servants to obey and to keep rules by their good will. Divine wisdom never makes people to do anything by force, or to serve or to worship by force.

Now, we are speaking on the Islamic rules and how we can practice them. Allah Almighty, from the beginning up to the end, when He sent His holy Message to the Last Prophet ﷺ, used His wisdoms, divine wisdoms, to teach people and to train them step by step, and Islam came into perfection, from its beginning up to its end, over a period of twenty-three years.

Now we are living fifteen centuries after Islam came, and Islam is clear. Nothing is secret in Islam concerning its rules. It is clear; it can be well-known and well-understood. And we are thanking Allah Almighty that in our time Islam is becoming more clear.

In our time, ideas or thoughts are so differing and opposing and specialized, and for each school of thought there is so much advertising; people are spending millions or billions for advertising their ideas. But Islam— no one is spending anything on it, nor on its ideas and principles, and yet Islam is becoming more clear. Anyone who looks at Islam can understand that, like a person looking at an artificial stone and at a genuine one.

It is now going to be understood that Islam brought conscious principles which it is impossible for a person who has a perfect view of them to reject, or for a person who has a perfect thought or idea when he looks at the Islamic rules. Therefore, we are not in need of advertising. Islam presents itself by itself to all people who have *'aqlun salim*, sound intelligence.

Therefore, in our days, only Islam is becoming more clear to everyone, and it is going to be more and more clear up to the time when Mahdi[81] comes, may Allah bless him. Then Jesus Christ will come, and Islam and its principles and rules will become clear to a perfect view. People now are interested, not a lot of people but even a few, and till those days come, we must see which rules or principles of Islam we must keep first.

I am seeing and hearing that so many Western people—learned people, also—are interested in Islam, but they are afraid of the Islamic rules, to put themselves under Islamic discipline. They are afraid because they are seeing Islam as a perfect system of rules and they are saying, "It is difficult for us to keep all the rules in Islam and to be a Muslim." And also our scholars, or Muslims who are doing Islamic *da'wa*, Islamic missionary work which is spreading throughout Western countries, are using a difficult method for everyone, and that makes people wonder about it. And most people are afraid to come under that Islamic discipline.

Therefore, as Allah Almighty says, *"La yukallif-Ullahu nafsan illa wus'aha'*[82]—Allah Almighty never loads on His servants more than they have the capability or capacity to bear. Then, when a person comes and wants to be Muslim, he asks, "How can I be Muslim? What is the entrance to Islam?" And we are saying, "The entrance is to say that I am witness to the existence and unity of Allah Almighty, and then I am witness that beloved Muhammad ﷺ is our Lord's servant and His messenger."

That is the main door by which we enter Islam. When a person says this, you must accept him as a Muslim. We can't take him out of Islam till he turns back and says, "I take back my words, I do not proclaim my witness to that." Then he takes himself out of Islam, apostasizes, and *then* we can say, "Now you are out of Islam." But for the main entrance, we are asking, "Do you accept the existence of Allah Almighty as your Lord?" and he says, "Yes." "Do you accept and do you witness that beloved Muhammad is His servant and His messenger?" and he says, "Yes." Then we say,

---

[81]The divinely-appointed leader who will come at the end-time of this world, as foretold in a number of *hadiths*.

[82](2:286)

"Come in." Then, if that person lives by it, keeping that *Shahadah*, that Witness, with himself, he is a Muslim, and if he dies, we wash his body and pray over it and bury it in a Muslim cemetery. Even if he does not keep any rule of Islam except this one, he is Muslim.

Then he can use that, the first principle among the pillars of Islam. The most important pillar is that one. Allah Almighty asks from everyone to proclaim that He is in existence and that He is One, and all the prophets are witnesses that they brought that first principle of Islam, that first pillar, to people. They came originally to make people proclaim the existence and unity of our Lord, and when we believe in their prophethood, we are affirming our *Shahadah*, our witness.

Yes, if you make that *Shahadah* with your tongue, it is going to be in your heart. If this whole building is full-up with coal and you put one burning coal into it, what do you think? That one burning coal can make the whole burn! Therefore, if a person accepts and says that Islam is my religion, and I am witness to the unity and existence of my Lord, Allah Almighty, and to beloved Muhammad ﷺ as His prophet and messenger and His servant, that is like a fire, burning the darkness, lighting the darkness in our hearts and burning the bad characteristics of our egos.

First, the Prophet ﷺ called people to proclaim the unity of Allah Almighty, and he said that I have been ordered not to put my sword in its sheath till people proclaim the unity of their Lord. This means that the main purpose of the Message of the Last Prophet ﷺ is to make people proclaim the unity of their Lord and His existence—calling people, and when they accept, that acceptance makes some feelings grow in their hearts, so that that person feels that I must respect that One who is in existence and who is my Lord, the Lord of the Heavens, the Lord of the worlds, the Lord of the children of Adam ﷺ.

When that feeling opens in a person's heart, then we may say to him, "If you would like to worship and to give your respects, most high respects, to your Lord, clean yourself." And even if he does not know the Islamic rules for cleaning, everyone knows to clean himself; everyone knows to wash his hands and his face and his mouth. But in Islam there is a rule concerning intention: you must intend, when you are going to do something, that I am doing this action to make my Lord pleased with me or I intend to do this action as a respect to my Lord. Intention is the difference between ordinary actions and Islamic actions. When you make such an intention, that is going to be an Islamic action. Without such an intention, it is an ordinary action.

And so you can clean yourself; it is a rule, an Islamic rule. If you do it once a day, it is all right, and if you want to do more, that is all right. And there are also rules for giving your most high respects to your Lord.

You can give your respect to a person by doing like this, doing like that, and those are the customs of people. But we are leaving customs and practicing *rules* because Islam is a religion and it has rules. Therefore, if you are asking how I can give my respect to my Lord, I may say that you can turn your face in the direction of your Lord's House in Mecca, and you can stand and can say, "*Allahu akbar*, my Lord is the Greatest."

If you say this, it is correct. And if you bow yourself out of respect to your Lord, it is correct, also. And if you put your forehead on the ground, that is the most humble action that a person can do toward anyone, and it is not for anyone except One. *You put your forehead on the ground in highest respect to your Lord.*

If you do that once a day, it is all right, and Allah Almighty is going to be pleased with you, also. The more you work or worship by means of your sincerity, the more Allah Almighty calls you to His Divine Presence. Therefore, inspirations are coming to your heart: "O My servant, come to Me again." It is good fortune for a person to be invited once more to his Lord's Divine Presence. If he has such an inspiration, he can do it again and yet again; as long as his Lord accepts his worship and calls him, he can do it. Then it is the best.

But the most important point, more than rules of worship, for every new Muslim, is that Allah Almighty is saying to him, "O My servant, I am accepting you now as a Muslim. You may do, out of respect for Me, as much as you can, but I am only asking from you to leave alone everything that is not good for yourself or for others."

That is important; Allah is asking *that*. And, *alhamdulillah*, I am seeing that every brother or sister who comes into Islam quickly leaves his or her past life's activities and quickly comes into the Islamic atmosphere. That is important, and it is the best action for any new Muslim brother or sister: to leave every no-good or bad action that he or she was accustomed to before coming into Islam, as Allah Almighty said through His Prophet, *"Tarku dharratin min maharam-Illah afdhalu 'ind-Allahi min 'ibadata-th-thakalain*[83]—to leave one unliked characteristic or unliked or prohibited action, is more lovely to Allah Almighty than the worshipping of all nations."

You can't do such worshipping as *that*. Yet if you could put all *um-mahs'*, all nations', all peoples' worshipping on one side of the scale and on the other side of it you put one bad thing that you are leaving of the bad characteristics or bad actions that you were accustomed to before coming into Islam, leaving that one bad thing is more lovely to our Lord than all the worshipping that all nations could do. It is sufficient as a proof that Allah Almighty likes that His servant should leave bad characteristics. Those bad characteristics are only our egos' characteristics, and Allah Almighty orders us to fight our egos so that we may leave every bad characteristic.

Therefore, if anyone wants to come into Islam, we have so many easy ways. And the Prophet said, also, *"Iman*, faith, has seventy three branches." If a person says *"La ilaha illa-Llah,"* accepting the existence and unity of the Lord, Allah Almighty, it is the highest form of faith to proclaim that. And the lowest degree, he said, is *"Imatata-l-adha min at-tariq,"* to remove anything that harms people in their path, like nails or thorns or banana skins or glass.[84]

Islam brings the most beautiful *adab*, behavior, and it is the sign of faith in the heart of that person. You can't say that the one who keeps such

---

[83]Literally, "To leave off the smallest bit of what Allah has prohibited is better in front of Allah than the worshipping of the two species [mankind and jinn]."

[84]Paraphrase of a *hadith* stating that *iman*, faith, has over seventy-three branches, the highest of which is to witness to the truth of Allah's existence and Oneness, and the least being to remove something harmful from the way.

ways[85] is an unbeliever; the Prophet says that he is a believer. Therefore, we may give rules to people or we may advise people to take what is easier for them from the rules of Islam, and it is all right. And *"Ajala-l-karamat dawama-t-tawfiq*[86]—the most important miraculous action for a person is to keep to something that he knows is best, not leaving it."

If you know that something is best or is the best way, you must keep it, not leaving it. Even though in our time it is so difficult to keep to the best thing that we know, maybe more difficult than holding fire in your hand, still you must be patient in keeping it. And we are asking forgiveness from Allah Almighty for everything in which we are guiding people into difficult conditions and making them to run away from Islam, although Islam is the easiest and most tolerant religion. ▲

---

[85]That is, someone who is sufficiently considerate and caring to remove what is harmful from people's path.

[86]Literally, "The most outstanding miracle is perseverance in following right guidance."

18: about avoiding dhulm

We must know for which thing Allah Almighty is going to be angry and which thing makes Him pleased with us because it has an effect on our personalities.

Every employee is too pleased when nothing comes on his record—too pleased, because if there is something on his record, it prevents him from rising. Everyone knows this. Then what about when we are servants? Why are you not asking which thing makes a bad record for ourselves in the Divine Presence? We must know.

Allah Almighty sent all the prophets, and through every *Shari'ah*—I mean to say, the ways that Allah Almighty established for His servants to walk on and to reach His Divine Presence—Allah Almighty made one prohibited thing common. There is one *haram* thing, a common *haram*, that is prohibited by Allah Almighty in every *Shari'ah*, through every message of His messengers. It is only one thing, never changing, and that makes Allah Almighty angry with His servants. *We must know!*

"Inni haramtu dhulma 'ala Nafsi"—Allah Almighty has made *dhulm*, cruelty, oppression, forbidden for Himself.[87] Then what about for creatures? On Judgment Day, if even the horn of a sheep has pierced another sheep, Allah Almighty will take vengeance for it from that one, for animals. Never is a person who does cruelty going to be left alone. Allah Almighty *must* ask from him and will avenge that person who has been wronged.

---

[87]This saying of the Prophet's is among those known as *qudsi ahadith*, a sacred *hadith* in which Allah Most High speaks about Himself by divine inspiration through the tongue of His Last Messenger.

That is the first and most important point that makes Allah Almighty angry with His servants: to be cruel. And what is cruelty [dhulm]? Everyone has a description of his own for cruelty; maybe you have a description. And Allah Almighty says to His servant, "O My servant, you know what cruelty is. According to what you know, you must keep yourself from that cruelty." Anyone can tell what cruelty is, and He is asking that, if you know what cruelty is, you must leave it, you must keep your ego from being cruel. That is important.

If you were to give a complete description of dhulm, there would be too wide an area for cruelty,[88] but it is not so important. Important is that, as you understand it, you must observe it. If you know that this is cruelty, you must keep yourself from that thing.

For dhulm, cruelty or oppression, we are giving a wide meaning, and it is, in short, to put something in a place that is not suitable for it. Yes. If you have a donkey and you put the donkey on your shoulders and go, it is dhulm because you must be on it, not it on you. You have put something in a place which is not suitable for it. You can put this carpet under your feet, you can't put it on your head—not suitable; you can be on this chair, you can't put this chair on your back. You must look at everything. If something is not in its right and suitable place, you are doing dhulm, cruelty.

You are putting women in the place of men. It is cruelty; to put a man in the place of women, that is cruelty. To throw iman, faith, out of the heart and to put kufr, unbelief, in the heart, that is cruelty. To look after yourself more than others, to think about yourself more than others, that is cruelty. So many things you may find that make you dhalim, cruel, and those things are dhulm, cruelty and oppression.

We are in need of divine protection here and Hereafter, we are in need of a shelter here and Hereafter. And through every prophet, in every message which Allah Almighty sent for His servants to be shelters for them, the first principle is to believe. Beliefs are shelters. To believe firstly in your Lord,

---

[88]Dhulm encompasses a number of broad meanings: misuse, iniquity, injustice, unfairness, oppression and wrong-doing

Almighty Allah, is the greatest belief, which keeps people here and Hereafter.

But Allah Almighty makes a condition for believers' faith to be shelters for them: if you are a believer, don't clothe your beliefs in cruelty, because a person may believe but at the same time he may use cruelty as a garment, dressing in cruelty. And that cruelty prevents that person from being sheltered under divine protection.

If you do not take care of what may harm other people, you may do so many bad things, and it makes you open to divine vengeance, because all the skies are full of the arms of vengeance. Don't think that if you do something, nothing will come on you—no! For everyone and for every action, there must be an effect in the Heavens; quickly it may be well-known which action is right and which must be punished. And the arms of divine vengeance are looking over people's actions; every action is under the eyes of those guardians in the Heavens who are keeping the whole world under their gaze, and quickly vengeance is coming upon those people.

Therefore, for every action you must be very careful. You must think about which thing you are intending to do, as sometimes those arms of vengeance are reaching your minds, coming from your thoughts, also. In everything, we are in need of intention, an intention to accustom, to train ourselves, an intention that keeps us away from troubles and from suffering, here and Hereafter. Therefore, in Islam, for every believer there must be good intentions.

Some people are coming to me and saying, "We have met with you and have listened, and we have seen that what you are saying is right." Then they are asking me if it is possible for us to follow you without coming into Islam; most of them are asking this. And I am surprised at people, why they are asking that. What wrong thing do they see in Islam that they are asking that?

Islam is one thing and Muslims are something else, because, if you speak truly, Islam remains in the Heavens, no longer on earth. It was a *huma*,[89] a precious bird which flew from our hands, and we are looking after it, like this. No more is Islam on earth; Allah Almighty has taken up that *Shari'ah*. So many nations of the Muslim world are saying now that the *Shari'ah* is no longer our law, and Allah Almighty is punishing them, taking the *Shari'ah* up. And so many times I am listening to our Muslim brothers here. They are saying that we must ask the British government to give us an opportunity or authority to bring the *Shari'ah* among ourselves. But you can't bring that. Allah Almighty has taken it away because we are not worthy of that *Shari'ah*.

Therefore, when people look at the Muslims living now, they are afraid to come into Islam or to be called Muslims, while to be Muslim is an honor in the Divine Presence. If it is not a good name among people in our day, still it is the most honorable name or most honorable title for servants in the Divine Presence. They *must* see that Islam orders people only to good actions and good intentions. If no good actions, a person is a cruel one, even though he may be Muslim; if no good intentions, he is a cruel one, even though his name may be Muslim.

Western people like to be realists; they are so proud of it. But they are *not* realists; "realist" is only a word they say, not *real* realists. If they were realists, they would realize what Islam is and what it means to be called a Muslim.

What is Islam? *Good actions and good intentions*, and we are not accepting bad actions for Islam, for Muslims, nor bad intentions, either. Therefore Allah Almighty orders, firstly, to make your intention when you come into Islam.

"La yu'minu ahadukum hatta yuhibbu li-akhihi ma yuhibbu li-nafsih."[90] That is an intention. You must correct your intention because a person who is not concerned or interested in others is a cruel person; an egotist is a cruel one, perhaps the most cruel one, like Pharaoh. Pharaoh represents all ego-

---

[89]A mythical bird.

[90]"None of you has believed until he likes for his brother whatever he likes for himself." (*Hadith*)

tism in himself, and he was the worst cruel one, tyrant. Therefore, Islam orders that, as the first step, you must clean your intentions and you must be clear.

If we had good intentions for others, we would not agree for anyone to be in *kufr*, in the way of falsehood. Therefore, Muslims struggled from the beginning because they did not accept cruelty or did not agree with the cruelty of people's saying that the Lord is not in existence or to say that we believe in idols.

Why did Muhammad ﷺ oppose those people? Was he a sadist? *Hasha*, God forbid! But they were *dhalimin*, cruel people, because they did not worship the Lord of the Heavens and the worlds; they gave their praises and respects to stone or wooden idols. Therefore he opposed them to take them away from that wrong-doing, that cruelty! But you are putting your ego in the place of your Lord and saying to it, "O my lord, as you like! What is your command?" and therefore we are cruel within ourselves.

Therefore, Islam is the best because, as the first step, if anyone bears witness and says, "I am witness to the existence of the Lord, Almighty Allah, and His unity," then he accepts and intends to give every right to everyone, as he gives to himself. Good intentions begin at the first step. If not, the Prophet ﷺ says, a person may be a believer, a Muslim, a *mumin* by name, but he has not yet reached, has not really put his foot in the true area of being in Islam. "Islam" is a most honorable title; *tuba*, highest good tidings, for those who can carry that title with honor. Allah gives honor to His servants by Islam, but Muslims—they should be punished now because they are making the name of Islam bad, while the name of Islam is in the Heavens.

That is our *dhulm*, our cruelty. Therefore, no more support for the Islamic world from Allah Almighty; no more divine support is coming for Muslims, because they are bringing down the name of Islam. We are the cruel ones. I am not ashamed of non-Muslims, no—but ashamed of our nation, of the Muslim world.

Therefore, when *dhulm*, cruelty, is going to reach the topmost point, Allah will send a Red wind[91] from East to West, from North to South, to take away everything. It is mentioned in *hadith*; I am not speaking from myself about that Red wind.

In Arabic, "red wind" also indicates hegemony; Red rulers, Red hegemony. A Red wind is coming from East to West, from North to South, covering the whole world. *"Wa tadhhaba rihukum."*[92] *Rih* means hegemony, power; *rihun hamran*, Red wind, that power which is taking over the whole world. That is a punishment for *dhulm*, for cruelty. When people are cruel individually, then collectively they should be put under Red hegemony, a Red wind, and punished here.

Therefore, everyone must think about himself, particularly in our days. We must clean our thoughts. That reactor [Chernobyl] burned, exploding, and people are trying to clean every place from that radiation. But look at the radiation in your head, in your thoughts! Red reactors' radiation is coming on thoughts, for all people. Even in the Islamic world, where people are saying that they are all right, that Red wind is coming through thoughts.

Make your thoughts clean from Red radiation. If even a little bit, you must be punished. That is important! Everywhere, in every country, people are becoming in two groups. Most people's thoughts are affected by Red winds. That is *dhulm*, cruelty, and that must be punished. Allah Almighty will never leave it.

Therefore, we must know which thing makes Allah Almighty angry with us. That Red 'radiation' makes our Lord angry! That is the first one; *that kills.* You may understand; we are not going to make it more than this. Those people may be angry but Allah's anger is on *them*. I am only saying this through my 'Headquarters.' You may believe, you may keep it in your heart.

And we are asking forgiveness for every bad thought and for every bad

---

91That is, communism.

92"And your strength departs." (8:46)

action which makes our names to be written on the cruelty list. Be careful, every day! Every night you must say, "*Astaghfirullah*, O my Lord. If my name is put on the list of cruelty, take it away." Otherwise, it is dangerous.

▲

19: the importance of respecting everyone

You must try to obey your Lord and you must try to give your love to your Lord. If a person does not give his obedience to his Lord, he is *dhalim*, cruel, and if a person does not give his love to his Lord, Allah Almighty, he is also cruel. Therefore, we must try to give our love to our Lord and to give our obedience to our Lord, Allah Almighty.

Why are we sitting here? We are here for one hour, or less or more. We want to keep people here in this assembly as long as we can because I am someone who has been authorized to address people and to call them to be obedient servants to their Lord and to give their love to their Lord; that is the purpose for which I have been authorized. Therefore, as long as I can keep you here, according to that authority, mercy is raining on you, and it is important to be under those mercy rains.

We know that practicing is difficult for everyone in our time because mostly people, and our egos, also, are calling us to be obedient to our egos, and our egos are also calling us to be obedient to devils. It is too difficult in our days to be obedient to the holy orders of our Lord, Almighty Allah, and now, as much as we can be far away from the outside world, we are sitting under a divine shelter and mercy rain is raining on people.

That is our gain because, when we go out, seventy devils are waiting for each one, to catch us and to take from us what we are carrying with ourselves, but we hope that we are gaining and taking from this assembly, from mercy rain. And we are giving them as an *amanah*, a trust, to our Lord, Allah Almighty, to keep them, and it is well-protected in our hearts, Allah Almighty protecting it.

Now, as we said, we are in need of practicing to be obedient servants and it is difficult, but we must carry difficulties because nothing can be gained without carrying difficulties. First, we must be patient, and we must try to learn *how* we can be patient. This holy month is teaching servants how they can be patient, and you must try. Fasting is a holy order from our Lord, Allah Almighty, for everyone.

The beginning of goodness and the beginning of good actions is intentions, and we must begin to be obedient servants through intentions. *You must intend!* And everyone has a tongue to say to his Lord, to address His holy Divine Presence, saying, "O my Lord, I intend to be Your obedient servant. Help me!" Then it is a good beginning. I don't think that Allah Almighty will refuse that from you, no.

Repeat it a second time, "O my Lord!" If a servant calls to his Lord, saying, *"Ya Rabb*—O my Lord," He promises to reply to His servant's addressing Him and He says, *"Labbayk!"* What is *"Labbayk"*? "Here I am," says our Lord to you.

Say it; you can talk. So much talking, each day; two angels are writing, each day filling so many books with your speech. *You can say this.* And all history begins from that addressing: "O my Lord! I am asking to be an obedient servant to You. Help me! I am asking to correct my intentions. O my Lord, help me! And I am asking to save myself from *dhulm,* from cruelty. Save me!"

And He says, "I am here. I will," He says. *"I will."* ("I will"—what does it mean? *"Muhaqqaq,* definitely!") "I am reaching to you," He says.

"Reach to me, O my Lord, with Your endless Mercy Oceans!"

"I will. I am reaching to you!"

When a ship is in danger, it sends an S.O.S. If you are asking for *najdah,* S.O.S., from your Lord, quickly, quickly, as much as you may be in need, His divine help reaches you. You can try.

But no need to try. *You must believe; you must believe.* And that is the key: only say, only ask. It is impossible for there *not* to be a reply. He *must* reply,

He *does* reply, our Lord. Say, "O my Lord, save me from the hands of devils," and He can save, He is able to save you from everything.

That is a good beginning. Then say, "I want, I intend, to fast," and He will send His divine support for fasting. So many little boys or girls here, also, among our assembly, are fasting; they are able to fast because they are intending, and their Lord gives them divine support for fasting. We have been asked to be obedient servants and we must ask for divine support.

Allah Almighty is asking from His servants to be respectful to Himself, and a part of being respectful to our Lord, Allah Almighty, is to be respectful to His servants. That is important. The twentieth century's people are very proud of the civilization of the twentieth century in which they have shares; each nation, particularly proud Western nations, is are proud of saying that it has a share in the twentieth century's civilization. But they have civilized themselves by technical means only; I do not see that they have civilized themselves by respecting nations or by respecting mankind. And we are saying this because each time a technological improvement occurs, I see that we are losing something of our humanity, and the more we look to technological improvements and means, the more we are going to be like those improved machines and to be robots; only moving, working machines we are going to be, without hearts. Therefore, that is a danger, or the most dangerous sign, for the future of mankind on earth, on this planet, on this *living* planet, and we must return to the beginning of our humanity. We must return to that point from where it began and we must begin our movement toward the horizon of humanity.

And when is it going to begin, what is the beginning? The beginning is going to be when you respect everyone who is one of the members of the great family of mankind. But we have lost that now, or we are going to lose it soon. Therefore, we are in need of a heavenly *mudakhalah*, intervention, to make people stop and to take away those technological improvements, because, for the sake of these technological means, we have lost our humanity. Therefore, when Mahdi comes, may Allah bless him and make us with him, he will say, "*Allahu akbar!* God is greater than even your technology. *Allahu akbar! Allahu akbar!*[93] and he will throw away all these technologies which are supporting the twentieth century's civilization. And we will say, *"Alhamdulillah!"* No more noisy sounds of cars or planes or trains or factories; yes, finished. "Oh, so restful," people will say. "No more running, rest!"

We are speaking about *dhulm*, cruelty. That cruelty is because of our intentions and our actions, causing people to be cruel. All human beings can now be put under the title of cruel mankind; believers and unbelievers, Muslims and non-Muslims, can now be called cruel.

What is the reason? Because people in the Muslim world are saying, "We are Muslims, we are believers in Islam, in our Lord's Holy Book, the Qur'an," but no one is practicing; therefore they are doing *dhulm*, cruelty. And non-Muslims, because they are fanatical people or too proud to look into the Holy Qur'an, the Last Message of our Lord, not looking at what it is but saying "No" to it, therefore *they* are cruel.

Therefore, Allah Almighty has opened to them a way through technology. They are not afraid of their Lord, but Allah Almighty is making them to fear from the technology which they have invented, trembling. They have built that reactor,[94] and now the whole world is trembling, using that machine, the Geiger counter. Allah Almighty is frightening all the world's people; no more control over that [nuclear reaction]. If it goes up, finished; impossible to be controlled because we can't order the wind, we can't order the rain, and wind and rain are taking radiation everywhere.

Therefore, we must turn back. We are walking too much on the wrong way; all humanity, all mankind, is on the wrong way. *"Don't enter!"*— there is a sign, "Prohibited Way," but all are running to it, till we *must* turn back.

Out of respect for our Lord, Almighty Allah, we must respect each other. When we go on *that* way, no one respecting the other, we are going

---

[93]According to *hadiths*, the Mahdi ﷺ will announce himself and his divinely-appointed mission by a threefold utterance of *"Allahu akbar! – God is Most Great!"*
[94]Chernobyl.

to share in what comes to them, no more humanity. And that is endless suffering for mankind in our time, even though we have everything and our life should be the happiest life among all the centuries. But it is going in the opposite way. The most suffering people are in our century, and if it continues to run at that speed and no heavenly intervention, then, by the beginning of the twenty-first century, all people are going to be crazy. No more time, only fourteen years! If there does not come a divine intervention, then all people, in East and West, from North to South, are going to be *majanin*, crazy ones. That is terrible!

Therefore, we are asking from everyone that, in our own capacity, we must learn to give respect to ourselves, beginning with our families, in our homes. We *must* do it; we must try to give respect to parents, to give respect to old people, to give respect to small ones, to big ones. In the family; we must practice it, and that is a sign of being obedient and respectful to our Lord. In the community, we must keep honorable people, and if you want to be honorable, you must give honor to everyone because Allah Almighty has given us an honor that He never gave to any other creature. He honored us, dressing us in honored deputies' garments and crowning us, also, with *takrim*, divine generosity, divine favors—everyone! But we are not keeping this.

We must keep it. And you must put an end to envy because envy takes away the respect of people for each other. The most dangerous illness for humanity is envy, and you must try to take it away.

It is a strange time now. Within in the family, you can see envy between husband and wife, and envy even in a huge way between male and female groups. All males are envious of females; females, also, have so much envy for males among themselves. Those people are saying, "You men have more rights," claiming that men are not giving them their rights, while Allah Almighty gives rights to them *and* to you. Always they are crying that they are *madhlum*, oppressed.

Envy—that is envy. The husband is envious of his wife, the wife envies her husband. Among children, brothers and sisters envy each other, neighbors to neighbors and employees to employees, the lower ones to the higher, wanting to reach that point and looking at the other with envy. It is the most dangerous illness, destroying humanity, and you must try to leave that. If you do not try, you will destroy yourself, plus all other people, because it is a fire.

Therefore we have been ordered to respect each other, and that respect takes away envy from ourselves. And we are asking forgiveness from Allah Almighty for everything, and particularly for being envious. It is not a good title for you, for a believer, to be envious; no, never! You must take it away, throw it out. ▲

20: keepinG islam's rules concerninG women

We have just arrived at the last day of Holy Ramadan, and we are sorry because the divine manifestations that belong to Holy Ramadan are going away; but a new month, a new moon, is coming, with a new mercy from Allah Almighty. And we are asking from our Lord, Almighty Allah, to let us reach many holy months like Ramadan during our lives, and to take more lights and more honor each time.

We know and believe that Islam is the best for everyone, individually and collectively, because Islam is perfect individually and collectively, and its rules are suitable for the nature of people. It is also perfect for the life of mankind on earth, and it is perfect, also, for our spiritual lives and for our spiritual development. It is excellent, so that no one can even imagine anything more perfect than Islam for developing people, individually and collectively, in their spiritual lives.

No one can bring any statement to that effect; anyone who can use his clean mind must recognize this. I must say "*clean* mind" because the twentieth century makes most people's minds dirty. They are saying "brainwashing," but it makes brains not washed but dirty about Reality, so that most people's minds are dirty and therefore they can't understand the real and true rules in Islam.

They are looking with black eyeglasses and seeing everything as black, and they are using them most of all for Islam and its rules. When they want to look at Islam, they are always putting on dirty eyeglasses, painted with black paint, so that anything at which a person may look after that he must see as a bad thing or with crooked lines on it. Therefore we are saying that people with clean minds, clean brains, who have not put up anything that prevents them from seeing the color and purity of Islam and its rules, can see that in Islam nothing is *'awaj*, crooked. Everything is straight.

And in our time, people are objecting or trying to accuse Islam most for its rules concerning women, and Western women are trying to accuse the rules in Islam about women most of all. But, as we said, they are fanatical people and they are always against Islam; they are always putting on dark eyeglasses painted with black coloring, which never show them what are the real rules and what the rules in Islam give to women.

In reality, Islam brought rules and rights for two kinds of people, rights for men and rights for women, and the Creator put those rules and rights for men and women, no one else. And you must know that men are created as men and women are created as women, male and female. It is impossible to say that men are equal to women or women are equal to men. Each kind of nature is just created as male or female, created in a special form. People must understand this.

It is impossible for men to wholly understand women's structure, and women also never understand what is the structure of a man. Men may be mistaken in the matter of giving rights to women and men may also be mistaken in proclaiming the rights of men, but Allah Almighty, as the Creator, knows what is perfect for men and perfect for women.

Some people are running after every evil, every bad thing, to make both sides, men and women, fall into sufferings or miseries. Therefore those people are saying to women that men are taking away your rights, are not giving you your rights. I am hearing these things in Europe, not in our countries in the Islamic world, although that is coming little by little to our countries, also; bad weather is coming. But here, I am surprised at how European women, Western women, are still not satisfied and they are saying that men are always cheating us, taking away our rights.

And I am with them, with women in Western countries. They have rights to complain and to accuse men because in Western countries the rules never keep the rights of women. That is true. Therefore I am with women in Western countries, because the rules are so bad in keeping the rights of women.

It is the biggest *dhulm*, cruelty or injustice, that has happened on earth to the rights of women to take women out of their homes and to put them among men, and force or oblige them to work as men work—*that* is cruelty! Those rules, all of them, are cruel because women were never created for outside work, but rather to be mothers, excellent mothers, excellent wives, excellent for their homes. And every crisis that is appearing on earth is for this reason, because of this point only.

Until women are going to be in their homes like queens, it will not change. Does Her Majesty the Queen go out and work anywhere, or only in her palace? And every woman must be in her house like a queen in her palace, but we men are not looking after them. The Islamic rules never say to leave women in chicken coops.[95] Never does Islam tell people to come and live on top of each other, to live our lives in such houses.

Yes, *ardu-Llahi wasi'ah*.[96] Allah Almighty is giving us a wide world for ourselves, such wide lands, wide countryside, and yet people are coming, one riding on the other in flats. They are making their lives in Hell here; yes!

Why are they all coming together? There can be so many towns, so many large spaces for building houses, big meadows or gardens, so that *that* queen can be like Her Majesty the Queen. She will never be without satisfaction—yes, such big gardens, such big houses; she would be happy there. But we are making such matchbox rooms, matchbox houses, and then ladies are saying, "We must go out. We must be pleased and enjoy ourselves by getting out."

And therefore, when Islam says something or gives a rule, if we practice it fully, everything is going to be on its right path. No one can say that a little girl growing up thinks of being a doctor or engineer or scientist or chemist or solicitor [lawyer] or officer or clerk or policeman. When a young girl grows up, it only goes through her mind to have a baby—a baby here, a baby there. Always dreaming, also—Allah knows well that they

---

[95]Referring to life in cramped city flats or apartments.
[96]"Allah's earth is spacious." (4:97, 29:56, 39:10)

dream of being good mothers, of having good husbands, of having good homes, and that is their happiness, that is their habit in general. If they are saying anything else, they are lying. Allah knows well!

Yes, they are growing up with that. Look! A little girl always takes dolls in her hand, doing like this, like that; Allah has put this among their characteristics. But we are fighting to change their characteristics, and we, men, are cruel. In particular, every rule that men have put in Western countries in the name of democracy, all of them are against the rights of women. And Islam just brings the true rights of women and says, "You are like queens and men are servants to you."

You must be servants to your wives! And the *Shari'ah*, Allah Almighty's rule, says that you must take care of your lady well, for eating, drinking and dressing, and she should look after you, because she is the only barrier between a man and Hells. If he has no wife, a person will fall into Hells; she is the barrier, and you must look after your wives as you look after your eyes. And she has been asked to keep your honor and to keep your descendants honorable, to look after their training, because every time it is the mother who trains the children. But now devils are taking the child from his mother and putting him in a nursery, fighting against natural rules, and Islam brings natural rules.

A mother must keep her babies close to her, like this. But it is coming to our countries, also; ladies are working. In the morning time, they are quickly awakening these little children and they may be crying, crying; taking them out, bringing them to a crèche, putting them there the whole day, and in the eveningtime coming and bringing them home, while that baby cries.

That is civilization? Even animals do not agree to have their young ones taken from them. *Then how do human beings, how mothers?* And they are saying that we are civilized people; all our rules are safeguarding women and their rights. And Islam says that you must keep your baby at your breast. *That* gives life to them, not throwing them into a crèche like lambs in a sheep pen. There are such places where they put ten, twelve, twenty of them, putting up a fence, and they are running around like this, like this, crying, doing everything on themselves. And what should that nurse do?

She says, "Leave them, they can die. The ones who had those children aren't looking after them. Then why should *we* look after them?"

Yes. Animals do not agree to leave their young ones. Look at cats, look at dogs, look at horses, look at donkeys, look at wolves, look at lions. Which of them leaves their babies? If anyone comes there, they rush at them, attacking. And we are human beings, yet we are saying that because this is the twentieth century's civilization, a mother must work!

Any woman who works gets no *barakah*, blessings, from the Lord for her money. Allah Almighty orders men to take care of the house, the family. We must not leave a woman, even if she has no husband, no parents, to work; the government must pay them to keep them in their homes. Maybe they can do something in their homes, but not among men, in factories or at any workplaces. And if a woman leaves, not looking after the home her husband provides, Allah Almighty takes away the *barakah*.

If only the man works and brings everything to his house, Allah gives more *barakah* and it is all right. We are seeing that if anyone makes his wife work, forcing her, and that woman brings something, all the *barakah* goes away; no blessings on them. Yes; if you don't have any need, why are you letting her go and work? Islam never accepts that, keeping a lady like a queen, and her husband to be servant to her and to her home.

This bad atmosphere is now coming to the Islamic world, and devils are saying that if women do not work, it is impossible to live; only one person's wages are not enough and women must work, also. It is a very wrong view. They may try to manage on one salary; they may try. But they are *not* trying. For everything we say, they are putting on black eyeglasses and saying, "No, it is not correct," and they are getting tired, and making women also to be more tired. If a man gets tired outside, he comes and sits in his home after work, but a woman must work outside and must work in her house, too, and that is cruelty. Therefore, no blessings on those people.

Allah Almighty is the Creator and He has put everything in its suitable place. Therefore, men cannot be women and women cannot be men. Women may be policemen in your countries (and in our countries they are beginning to do that, also), but sometimes I am saying, "Since they are saying, 'We are policemen, you are policemen,' let the lady police look after London for one night while we are sleeping in our houses, if they are able to take care of this city!"

Yes, we must take care of *them*. Allah made each kind, male and female, in their specialized positions. This was just created for *this* purpose, that was created for *that* purpose. Men were created to be fathers and the servants of their homes.

We are saying "servants" but devils are saying that man is the chief of the family, *sayyid*, and that women are second, and that is a big lie. Allah Almighty made man the servant and protector of ladies, not the chief but the protector and the servant to the family. But devils are changing that, saying, "No, you women are down and men are up."

That is a big lie, making every family upset, and then wife and husband are becoming like two roosters: "I am the rooster!" "No, *I* am the rooster!"—like this, everywhere in Western countries, and in Eastern countries that illness is also coming, little by little. In our countries women are still saying, "We are hens. It doesn't matter if you are the rooster," and then they are happy, satisfied, no more quarreling. But the illness of the twentieth century's civilization is running into the Islamic world, and I am sorry.

Each time we are leaving the correct rules, the natural rules that Allah Almighty has put for mankind, we are falling into miseries and sufferings. Allah Almighty is saying, "I do not want My servants to be in miseries or to suffer," but we are saying, "No, we like to suffer." And then Allah Almighty says, "You are free. As you like, do." If you do not say to your Lord, "O my Lord, as *You* like," He says to you, "O My servant, as you like you may live, but don't complain." And the whole world now is complaining; rich countries, poor countries, industrial countries and farming countries—all are complaining.

The reason is that we want to live as we like, not as *He* likes; all people want to live as they like. Yes, *you* know—when a young person escapes from his or her parents, saying, "I must live my life; no more control from you on me." Isn't it so? Every young person is saying this and escaping from parents, in flats, in rooms. They are saying, "I must live my life!"

Yes, you may live your life, but it is so dangerous and terrible, finally. It is a new fashion, the Devil's rules, to make people unhappy, to make them in sufferings. A young kid comes out and looks, and Satan puts eyeglasses on him which make everything look pink—a pink world, rose-colored glasses, which make kids run away. "You are big now; enough control from your parents. You must live your life and run!" Satan is putting those glasses on them, but then so many are coming and crying to me, also. Each day so many are coming, my "customers"—so many, so many, complaining about their kids, about youth. What can you do? Nothing; finished!

Therefore, Islam brings every rule suitable for nature; you can't find any rule in it against nature. It is suitable because the Creator of nature and the Creator of the natures of people is our Lord. He knows what is the best. But we are saying, "*I* know! I must live my life."

Yes, you may, but you are living against nature, and whoever lives against nature, nature punishes him by the order, by the command, of Allah Almighty. No mercy on those people from nature; no, not at all. They must be punished. Physicians are saying, "No, we can't do anything. Because you are being punished by nature, we can't do anything; finished!" You like it? Then if you like it, you may live as you like. If you don't like that, you must say, "O my Lord, as *You* like, I am intending to live a clean life, an honorable life, a happy life, with pleasure."

And that is all. We must understand Islam and its rules. You must look at the rules of Islam, and whatever thing is not suitable for nature, bring it to me. But the one who puts on black eyeglasses, he can't see it.

Then take your eyeglasses away; don't be fanatical. From London I am addressing all nations from East to West, from all mankind, to look at the rules in Islam. If they want to save themselves here and Hereafter, if they want to live an enjoyable and happy life here and Hereafter, they must look at the rules in Islam, both men and women, and not be fanatical. ▲

21: concerning sayyidina khidr, the greatest holy name and *lailat al-qadr*

We have arrived at the last part of Holy Ramadan, and it is the most precious part of Holy Ramadan because the Night of Power is in it. And we have been ordered to look for that precious night, the most valuable night for Muslims during the whole year.

Allah Almighty hides His Greatest Name, and He hides *Lailat al-Qadr*, the Night of Power, and He also hides Khidr 鍼, the Green Man;[97] these three things are hidden. Allah Almighty wants His servants to be respectful to everyone so that some time you may find that Green Man, Khidr 鍼, because he has the power to give you happiness and peace here and Hereafter. He has the most powerful spiritual dress, and he can give it to anyone who can meet him.

But it is not easy to find him. Anyone who is asking truly one day must find him, must meet him, but he may come through any figure, may appear in any form of a man—sometimes as an old man, sometimes as a young man; sometimes with a beard, a long-bearded one, sometimes without a beard; sometimes as a poor man, sometimes as a rich man. You never know.

Allah Almighty honored the children of Adam and He is asking from you that you give honor to each other, also. But people in our time are only looking to see if a person has a good outward appearance, giving greetings

---

[97]A reference to that "servant among Our servants to whom We had granted mercy from Ourselves and had taught him, from Ourselves, knowledge" (18:65)—that is, Sayyidina Khidr 鍼, whose story is told in 18:65-82. He is traditionally associated with the color green.

and respect. That is the twentieth century's 'civilization,' not *real* civilization.

Those who are looking only at our outward appearance, they are not civilized people. Civilized people must really see a person as a member of mankind and must give their respect. Don't say that that is a black one, that is a colored one, that is a Turkish one, that is a Pakistani one, that is an English one, that is a Russian one—no, because all of us, we are members of a huge family. Allah Almighty made mankind as a family, a big family, and we must respect and we must support each other.

Therefore, the most precious one, who is able to live throughout centuries, at the time of Moses and before and after, he is living. Sayyidina Khidr lives, and if a person meets him, he must reach happiness and peace here and Hereafter. But Allah Almighty has made him to be secret so that we may give everyone respect. That person may be Khidr 🕮, or this one or that one. When you keep that respect, one day you *must* meet him.

And second, Allah Almighty has hidden the Greatest Name, *Ism al-A'dham*. He has ninety-nine Holy Names; one of them is *Ism al-A'dham*. Whoever makes *du'a*, supplication, with that greatest Holy Name, Allah Almighty quickly gives him what he asks. If a person were to know it, he would quickly make *du'a*, but Allah Almighty hides that Name so that you may give respect for every Holy Name, because that divine manifestation burns all the other ninety-nine Holy Names. And sometimes the greatest Holy Name may be with another Holy Name—for example, *"Allahu Rahman," "Allahu Ghafur," "Allah Karim,"*[98] coming with that one and hiding it to create a respect for every Holy Name of our Lord, Allah Almighty.

And thirdly, Allah Almighty hides the greatest night, the holiest night in Islam, the Night of Power, *Lailat al-Qadr*. Whoever wants to take power over his ego, over his enemies, *dhahir wa batin*, outward or inner enemies[99]— whoever wants that power, to be a real deputy of Allah Almighty not only

---

[98]Allah the Merciful, Allah the Forgiving, Allah the Generous.

[99]"Inner enemies" refers to *nafs* (the ego or lower self), Satan, *dunya* (worldly attractions) and *hawa* (the base desires of the lower self), as explained in many of Shaykh Nazim's talks.

on earth but also throughout the universe, he must take care to reach that Night, the Night of Power. And Allah Almighty hides it, also, so that you may not depend that it is going to be fixed like *Lailat al-Bara'at* or *Lailat al-Me'raj* or *Lailat al-Maulid* of the Prophet 鬱.[100]

You may find it amongst all the nights of the whole year, but mostly Allah Almighty puts it in Ramadan, also making it during the last ten nights of the last one-third of Ramadan, from His endless mercy making us to find it easily in the last third. And the Prophet 鬱 also indicated that there may be another easy way to find it, saying that you may find it amongst the last ten odd-numbered nights of Ramadan, like the twenty-first, twenty-third, twenty-fifth, twenty-seventh, twenty-ninth, and then, to make it still easier, saying that it mostly comes on the twenty-seventh night.

Be ready, be careful. Perhaps for that opening you may be there, to see that power coming on you, dressing you in that *nur*, light, for that Night, giving you an endless power. And we are asking forgiveness for you, for me, for all Muslims, and for all the children of Adam. ▲

---

[100]These are other holy nights of the Islamic year. *Lailat al-Bara'at*, observed on the night between the 14th and 15th of the month of Sha'ban, is the occasion when the accounting of one's life and sustenance for the year is taken by Allah, and those who merit it are blessed with divine forgiveness. *Lailat al-Isra' wal-Me'raj*, the Night of the Journey and the Ascension, is the night of the 27th of Rajab during which the Holy Prophet was miraculously transported to Jerusalem *(al-Isra')* and then to the Seven Heavens and the Divine Presence *(al-Me'raj)*. *Lailat al-Maulid*, the night preceding the 12th of Rab'i al-Awwal, is the Prophet's birth night.

22: the importance of avoiding bad actions

We are the children of Adam, from the beginning up to the end, and we have activities, actions—yes? And the Prophet ﷺ said, "*'Amalukum 'ummalukum.*"[101]

What the Seal of the Prophets ﷺ said is true; he was speaking the truth, the absolute truth. How could a person who said *"An-najatu fis-sidq, the salvation of mankind is in truthfulness,"* speak falsehood? *"An-najatu fis-sidq"*—safety or salvation is in being truthful. No one harms himself by being truthful or being a true one, but whoever leaves truth must be harmed here and Hereafter. And the Prophet ﷺ, the most truthful one who ever lived, said, " *'Amalukum 'ummalukum."*

We have activities or actions, *'amal;* everyone has activities for each day. When we die, no more activities, but as long as we are alive we are in activity, and everyone must look after his activities or actions. There are satanic actions or activities and *rahmani*, divine or heavenly or holy activities. And everyone must be either with these or with those activities or actions.

Now we are in an activity here. Each day in Holy Ramadan we have activities. We are trying to make our activities or actions during this holy month heavenly activities, good activities, so that our Lord, Almighty Allah, is pleased with us, and we are seeing that such good activities are filling our days; during this month we are giving only a short time for other activities and mostly we are coming to do heavenly activities. And when we are doing heavenly activities, quickly we can find positive results on our hearts and on our minds and on our physical bodies. These three kinds of reactions

---

[101]"Your works [actions, activities] are your workers [that work for you]."

may be seen from our heavenly activities during this holy month—benefits, yes?

And Allah Almighty, from the first messenger up to the last, gave orders to His servants, and prohibitions, also, ordering them to do some things and to leave some other things. In every religion, through every prophet, it comes: good activities or actions that He orders and bad activities or actions that He prohibits, nothing else. And Allah Almighty speaks divine wisdoms in ordering some actions, and for some others which He orders us to leave, He speaks wisdoms, also.

I am saying two words in Arabic; perhaps they may be translated into two words in English, also. Allah Almighty ordered worshipping to His servants, saying, "O children of Adam, I have ordered for you good actions and worshipping *li-karamatika*, to make you more honorable. When I order you to do something for worshipping, I want to give you more honor, more lights—*li-karamatika*."

When we are praying, Allah Almighty takes away every evil from ourselves. There are angels. If a servant comes to worship his Lord, angels take those no-good things from him, and, when he is going to stand in the Divine Presence, from the Divine Presence come garments of *nur*, garments of honor, because we have been invited to be in the Divine Presence. And that is honor.

People in our time are running away. They are saying, "It is too much to pray every day." But if every day Her Majesty the Queen invited you, would you say that it is too much, or would you run like a horse to accept that invitation? Yes. And for Allah Almighty, when He is asking worshipping. from us, He wants to give more honor to us by His orders, because to keep your Lord's orders gives you more honor and more respect in the Divine Presence, and as long as you are a worshipper and as long as you are respectful to your Lord, Allah Almighty, then Allah Almighty makes respect for you. You are going to be respected among creatures; from everything, from everyone, may come to you respect because Allah Almighty is clothing you in respect from His Divine Presence.

Therefore, for all activities or actions which are heavenly activities, the purpose, the aim, is to give us more honor, and you are going to be designated among all creatures as an honorable servant and their dealings with you are going to be with respect. As much as you give respect, you receive, in the face of it, more respect.

Therefore, " *'Amalukum 'ummalukum.* " Everyone who deals with you, the Prophet is saying, deals with you according to your actions, whether bad or good. If your activities or actions are respectful to your Lord, then everyone's dealings with you must be respectful, and if in your dealings with your Lord your activities are bad, then everyone's dealings with you must be bad, with no respect for you.

At the same time, Allah Almighty is also preventing or prohibiting His servants from certain activities, and He says to the children of Adam, with divine wisdom, *"Ya bani Adam, nahaitukum an ashya bi-salamatika. Ta'at bi-karamatika, wa anni nahaitukum 'anhum bi-salamatika,*[102] I am prohibiting to you things for your safety." *Bi-salamatika* means to keep you away from harm. "Everything that harms you, I am making that prohibited."

Look at everything, if you have a mind. If it is empty you can't think, but if you have something in it, you can understand that the thing which Allah Almighty prohibits must be something that harms you. And every bad activity or action harms you, either in your body or in your mind or in your heart. *Must be!* If nothing comes to your body from it but your heart is in trouble, you must suffer after that prohibited activity. Therefore, the *hadith* of the Prophet ﷺ, " *'Amalukum 'ummalukum,*" says, "O people, according to your activities or actions you are reaching some results, either harming you or making you pleased. Therefore, you must look after your actions always."

If they are satanic, those satanic actions are not easy to leave because our *nafs* likes them. That is the trouble. Our *nafs* never likes heavenly ac-

---

[102]"O children of Adam, I have prohibited to you [certain] things for your well-being [or safety]. Obeying [them] is for your honor and that I have prohibited you from them is for your well-being [or safety]."

tions or activities, always wanting to be in satanic activities, and each time your ego calls you to a bad activity, it is very happy with that. But afterwards you are going to think about it because something, some punishment, will come to you, whether you are thinking about it when you are in it or you are thinking about it in the future. So many people, for some bad activities, are crying throughout their whole lives. No science can take it away from that one, nor riches nor ranks nor knowledge; *nothing* can take from him the reaction to the bad action that he did. And it may be only for some minutes or for some seconds, but because of that bad action, he or she should cry for a whole lifetime.

You may understand, you may know, what bad activities people are running after, males and females running after those bad activities that Allah Almighty has prohibited, and no one asking if it is good or not. They are only running without thinking, without using their minds, running into that current, and whoever falls into it, it carries him or her away. It is now called "freedom," freedom in everything, freedom without limits.

Those are satanic activities in our time which people later regret too much, but it is useless, gone by. Therefore, Allah Almighty is saying, "O people, I do not want you to fall into sufferings. I am pulling you away from troubles, but My servants are running into the fire as a moth to a flame."

A moth flies into the fire and fire burns, and people are running into the fire but they can't see the flames. Our world is now burning with fire, with flames, and we are seeing it, from East to West, from North to South. Every place is amidst fires.

Muhiyuddin ibn al-'Arabi, may Allah bless him, was saying, "Day by day, when the last days approach, a fire is going to blaze on earth, everywhere, little by little, because everyone will take a match to kindle that fire—*everyone!*"

Satan was created from a flame of fire; therefore he likes fire too much, and he also likes to burn people by his fire. Therefore he is teaching people everything that has to do with fire. Before there were no firearms, but he taught them to make weapons which work with fire, and the whole world now, all nations, are racing with each other, arms race, to make them more and more. Satan is very happy, giving everyone a match. A match is a small thing, but there is a chain reaction, putting the nuclear match everywhere and saying, advising people, "You must do more and more." Even one is enough to make the whole world in flames but he is saying, "No, not enough yet! They must *all* be there."

And Muhiyuddin, a king-sized *wali*, saint, was given telescopic eyes to look into the future, telescopic eyes for looking into the Holy Qur'an, for looking into holy *hadith*. The one who looks into them may see what is coming in the future, but blind people, even if you put a telescope or microscope in front of them, never see anything. And *awliya*, saints, are looking and seeing what is coming, and Muhiyuddin was saying that this is approaching. When the last days come near, a fire is going to burn over all the world, even blazing on the seas.

Now *awliya* are seeing that everywhere people are running into fire, men and women. Each prohibited action is making another flame and people are running into it. Then how can you stop suffering? Money can stop sufferings? No! We have everything, but sufferings are mounting because everyone is adding another flame to this fire.

Nimrod ordered his nation to bring more and more wood to burn Abraham 安. For what? Nimrod wanted to burn not Abraham 安, because only one match is enough to burn a person, but his intention, his aim, was to burn *tawhid*, faith—to take it off the earth. Therefore he commanded his people, saying that whoever wants the highest rank in my presence must bring more wood to burn.

It was a huge hill of wood which the people brought. From Basra in Iraq, when it was burning, the flames could be seen in Damascus. And now Satan is making people gather to build a big fire. Everyone is working for Satan to make a flame, also, and he is asking them, "Burn faith, burn beliefs," so that no one is going to be a believer on earth. *That* is his aim now.

The Prophet 鬱 says, "There is a *jawhar*, jewel, but there is something which makes that *jawhar* worthless." And religion or beliefs, they are jewels. What makes them worthless is fornication; *that* makes beliefs worthless.

And everywhere now Satan and his workers are doing advertising for every kind of fornication, and everyone is striking this match, making a fire from East to West.

That is dangerous! No more *karamah*, no more honor, remains with people; *that* burns it. That is the meaning of what Muhiyuddin ibn al-'Arabi, may Allah bless him, was saying. Day by day, it is going to cover the whole world with flames. At the least, these eyes are doing fornication—*at the least*, and that burns faith and beliefs. If a nail comes into the tire of a car, puncturing the tire, then quickly that car will stop; it can't go on. Even one, one glance, does the same thing to faith, to beliefs.

When you are approaching the Divine Presence, that glance makes you stop immediately. You must come down, you must see whether you have a spare or not. If you have one spare, you can remove that punctured one, putting the spare, but after a little bit comes another, and no more spare. Sometimes it comes for all four tires at once and then goes down—yes!

Therefore, in our time, improvement, spiritual improvement, is so difficult. Everything that we may gain from spiritual practices is quickly runs out through our eyes and we remain behind. Therefore it is impossible, without locking the doors of fornication by every means, to take away suffering from people or to give spiritual improvement; it is too difficult. You must take along too many spare tires; one second's looking puts you on the ground. Then what if you go up in a plane and one engine becomes destroyed? If you move from the earth, it is so terrible if you have something wrong; yes. We are still on earth; doesn't matter, falling, getting up. But we are asking for the Heavens, we do not want to be always on earth.

We have been invited, and the time is approaching and flames are covering the whole world. Bad activities are covering from East to West, and you must look after yourself, to take some precautions for yourself. You must be able to understand which activities satanic deception is coming through; you must be very careful.

I am asking forgiveness for my sisters, for my brothers, for everyone, and asking from our Lord, Almighty Allah, for His divine help in sending us someone to lock up every door that is open to fornication and that takes away honor from mankind. They are saying "girlfriend" or "boyfriend," and I am asking, "This is a friend, or your wife? This is your friend, or your husband?"

Why are you not making it legal but are always going on illegally? What is the reason? You are accepting that girl, you are accepting that boy; then, after accepting, what is the meaning of doing that illegally? But—bad activities, Satan advising them, "Keep this one for some days and then leave her, leave him, and go to another one."

That is not honor for mankind. It is not written in any of our holy books, from the beginning up to today. These bad activities are the harvest or the product of our times, the product of the twentieth century's civilization—badness, dishonorable things. A father sees his daughter bringing a man. "Who is this one?" "My boy friend." Or his son brings someone. "Who is that one?" "Girl friend, my girl friend." *"My son's girl friend!"* And then they are saying, "All right, all right." That is not honor for parents but is finishing honor!

We are asking forgiveness from Allah Almighty, and we are asking Him to send someone from His Divine Presence with divine powers to stop that. Therefore, our "Headquarters" is advising, we are advising, our brothers and sisters not to be single, not to be unmarried; *must be married.* That is a safety and honor for ourselves in our time, and it is the beginning of spiritual improvement. Without marriage, it is too difficult. ▲

23: being pleased with allah almighty

By the name of Allah, All-Mighty, All-Merciful, Most Beneficent and Most Munificent. You can't find anyone who can be more merciful to mankind than their Lord. We may be sinners but yet our Lord is merciful to us; we may be disobedient people but yet He sends from His endless favors to ourselves—yes. And He is asking from His servants to say, "Thank You, O our Lord," but we are too greedy to say it.

If you say "Thank You," He will not leave you without giving you anything; as long as you say "Thank You," He will pour on you more and more. Therefore, *Wa-shkuru Li*. *La'in shakartum, la-azidannakum*. My servants, if you thank Me, then I will give more and more to you."[103] But you are forgetting Me. When you forget, I am leaving you as forgotten. I do not forget anyone, but as a punishment to you when you forget Me, I am leaving you as someone forgotten."

He gave us the key of happiness but we are not using it. Our Lord just gave us it, and that is the key: *"La'in shakartum, la-azidannakum.* If you thank Me, I am going to give you more and more."

For which thing are we giving thanks? If you receive a favor from someone, you say "Thank you" because you are pleased. That is happiness, and when you are happy, you must say "Thank you." And Allah is saying, "If you feel happiness, you must say, 'O my Lord, thank You because You are making me happy and making me pleased,'" and then He is going to increase His favors on you more and more.

---

[103] "And be thankful to Me." (2:152) If you are thankful, indeed I will grant you increase." (14:7)

You may say, "What about the difficult conditions which people or society or all mankind have fallen into, such bad and difficult conditions—how can I be happy or in peace?" But Allah Almighty has endless ways to make His servants happy and pleased with Him. When you choose the way of thankfulness, it leads you to an area of pleasure, to an area of happiness, and anything may happen but that never changes your happiness.

The prophet Joseph, Yusuf, the son of Jacob, peace be upon them both, was thrown into a well. It was a terrible well, but Allah Almighty sent the angel Gabriel to Joseph to give his Lord's greetings to him and bring him good tidings about his future, saying, "O My servant, I am pleased with you. Are you pleased with Me?"

And Joseph said, "O my Lord, if *You* are pleased with me, what must be my pleasure? I may be in a well, but in reality I am in Paradise when You say 'I am pleased with you.'"

That well might be full-up with snakes, lizards, scorpions and spiders all around. No worry for him; he was pleased with his Lord! Nothing could harm him because he was pleased with his Lord, and his Lord asked if you are pleased with Me, because I am pleased with you. And then Allah Almighty sent around a group of people to take Yusuf out, quickly taking him from the well and arriving in Egypt, the country of Pharaoh. And he was pleased; anywhere he might go he would be pleased.

That is one key that makes you happy throughout your life. Allah Almighty, every day, every morning and evening and at every time, is asking you, "O My servant, are you pleased with Me?" But our ears—people are putting cotton inside; only that, listening to nothing.

Allah Almighty is looking at His servant: "O My servant, are you happy with Me, are you pleased with Me?" And what are you saying? Yes; He is asking His servants and He is seeing whether they are pleased with Him. But mostly, if He were asking and we were listening, so many people would reply, "How am I going to be pleased with You? No money," they would say. "So many people are poor. So that we can have more money, let this rain rain down silver coins. *Then* we will be happy!"

A person was complaining that he hadn't any shoes. But one day he saw a man with no legs, and he said, "O my Lord, I am very happy, O my Lord! Very peaceful, my life. I am so happy, so pleased with You, O my Lord." When he saw that no-legged person, he understood what he had, which thing he had been given. Yes, no more asking or complaining about shoes. That doesn't matter because I have legs, but *that* person—no legs.

Do you not see blind people? Who would give up his two eyes? If I give this whole place full-up with gold, would anyone give even *one* eye? Yes, what rich people we are! If I give you the whole world, to be king of it but without eyes, will you accept? If these eyes are closed, what is the taste of life without seeing? You will be a blind king. *Alhamdulillah*, we have eyes. We are rich ones, yes!

Therefore, when we are looking at our Lord's favors, we must be happy. But we are asking something from our Lord, Almighty Allah, which is too cheap; the cheapest things we are asking for. We must ask from our Lord, from His endless favors, something that will be ours forever.

Each thing that you are asking of this world and of this life, it is temporary. Nothing is going to be permanent except the heavenly grants that Allah Almighty is granting to you. *You must ask!* Heavenly grants are going to be with you forever, and He likes His servants to ask for something that is valuable.

The Holy Qur'an is teaching people through many tales. Allah Almighty is giving examples from passed-away nations and their life conditions, and is teaching us.

Don't be like the Children of Israel! Allah Almighty put them in the Desert of Sinai. Then, when they were imprisoned there, each day Allah Almighty sent them, from the Heavens, *mann wa salwa*.[104] That is very beau-

---

[104]These two foods, provided for the Israelites during their wanderings in Sinai, are mentioned in the Holy Qur'an are mentioned in three verses, which read, "And We sent down to you manna and quails, [saying], 'Eat of the good things with which We have provided you'" (2:57, 7:160 and 20:81). *Manna* (the manna of the Bible) is a sweet, sticky substance coming

tiful, too delicious food; people regard *kebap* as delicious.[105] Each day He was sending those birds, very tasty, delicious, and *halwah*, that sweet—each day.

Then they said to Moses, "What about this *kebap* and that sweet every day? Every day, in the morning, this sweet, and at nighttime *kebap*, or in the morning *kebap* and in the evening the sweet. We are fed-up! Ask from your Lord for something like onions, garlic and cucumbers—something like that. We are fed-up with this, every day *kebap* and sweet!"

Look what they were asking from Allah Almighty—and we are like those people, also, the same characteristics. We are asking, "Give us more of this life's pleasures." And you know that from the time of maturity, from that day, your pleasures are making a path from maximum to minimum, coming down. No one is going to have the same taste from the beginning of maturity to the end of his life. As much as you are asking, you are given, but its taste is going to be less day by day, day by day, day by day.

Why are you asking for *that*? You must ask for something valuable in the Divine Presence for yourself! He gives; He is not stingy. Generosity is His attribute, the divine attribute of your Lord, Allah Almighty. He gives. Ask; He can give! And say, "O my Lord, I am asking from You that I may be pleased with everything that You are giving to me."

One day a black fellow was walking with his boss in a garden. Colored people, Allah gives them more *barakah*, blessings. We don't have that, but, to any house that a colored person is in, Allah Almighty sends so much *barakah*. Therefore, in earlier times everyone had colored people in their houses, in their farms, and Allah sent more *barakah*. The Prophet said it. We must like them—yes.

They were going though fields that were planted, and his *sayyid*, master, cut a cucumber. It was so bitter that he made a face at his servant. But his

---

from trees, found to this day in Iraq, Iran and other parts of the Middle East, and *salwa* is quail.

105That is, the quails were cooked as kabobs.

servant ate it, all of it. "Isn't it bitter?" his master asked.

He said, "O my master, so many times I have eaten sweet things from your hand. Why does it matter if once you give me something bitter? I am ashamed to throw it away because it is coming from your hand to me."

This is a big lesson for those people who have minds or have hearts. Our Lord is sending us endless favors and we are receiving them, but if sometimes something comes upon ourselves, we are complaining about our Lord. He never likes complaining, and no happiness or pleasure for the one who opens the door of complaining.

Believers must not complain. That is the key of happiness. There are some people whose habit is always to complain. Look! You may find such people and you never find them any day without complaining. Therefore, all the prophets advised their companions, their people, not to complain. And our Prophet ﷺ lived in the desert. He was born in Mecca amidst huge deserts, hot weather and no water, no trees, no plants. And his Companions always suffered because of little food, but no one complained. They would fast, and mostly they would make their breakfast with two or three dates. (When we are sitting, before eating dinner, thirty dates, like a machine. *Yahu!*[106] While I am eating one, other people are eating ten!) Yes. They got one or two dates, or even a half, but they did not complain.

Therefore, Islam has a strong base. The Companions of Muhammad ﷺ were strong enough to bear every difficult condition, particularly being hungry. Many times they would show that they were putting stones on their stomachs to keep away the pain of hunger, and the Prophet showed that he sometimes had *two* stones. And we have been given everything but *still* we are complaining. Therefore, no pleasure for the one who complains.

Therefore Islam and its Holy Book begin by saying *"Alhamdulillah."* O people, you must always say *"Alhamdulillah."* It means "All praise and all thanks to You, O our Lord" when you say it. If a person does nothing except to say *"Alhamdulillah, alhamdulillah, alhamdulillah . . ."* from the begin-

---

[106] A Turkish expression, meaning approximately, "My goodness!"

ning up to the end of his life, it is enough. If he says, "O my Lord, I can never find time, I can't do anything except to say '*Alhamdulillah, alhamdulillah.*' I am never going to be unoccupied with it, so that I can't do anything of worshipping except saying '*Alhamdulillah, alhamdulillah, alhamdulillah . . . ,*'" it is enough.

For every condition, you must make ready "*Alhamdulillah,*" and then every difficulty goes away; it brings solutions for every difficult problem. Just only one way; try it—I am advising you. Leave off complaining and say, "Thanks and glory be to Allah Almighty," because He is sending us endless favors, and if sometimes something difficult comes on us, it is no good to complain. When you complain, Allah Almighty says, "Look at My servant, complaining about Me to My other servants," and it is no good to let your Lord say this; *it is no good.*

Therefore, the keys of happiness are in our hands; He gave them. This is the tradition, from the first prophet up to the last one. Don't suppose that this is only the Last Prophet's advice, but from the beginning up to the end, through their traditions (and we have been sent 124,000 prophets), all the prophets were calling to people, "O people, be pleased with your Lord. Be happy with Him, be respectful to Him, and He will make you pleased, here and Hereafter." ▲

24: Good intentions, the key to Goodness

Islam means truth, *haqq*. And if we would like to be with *haqq*, we must follow and we must accept Islam.

We have not come to this life to play. It is a serious thing that we are here, and we have been ordered to know what is truth and we have been ordered to know what is falsehood, and to choose between them.

We must keep with truth, but truth is bitter for our egos. They like falsehood; falsehood is lovely for our *nafs*, so that it is difficult for a person to choose between truth and falsehood. But if you use your mind, it should say to you, "Keep to the safe way. Choose the truth."

Prophets and *awliya* are the leaders of this caravan which is going toward Allah Almighty; they are moving from this life and their direction is toward Allah. They are those people who never look at or are interested in this life's cheap pleasures. They know what is valuable, and they are joined to that caravan that has been moving since the first man and the first prophet, Adam ﷺ.

He began when he was sent on earth. He was longing to return to his homeland, Paradise, to his Lord's Divine Presence, and he began as the first one in the caravan moving toward Allah Almighty, and he called his sons, his children, to follow him.

The ones who accepted followed him from the time that that caravan moved, and when his children left off following the caravan, Allah Almighty sent another prophet, another beloved one from among His servants, to call people to follow the caravan. And those who accepted the prophets followed it. But there is another caravan, led by Satan, and he is also calling people to his caravan.

Those who are following the prophets are coming with them toward Allah Almighty and His Divine Presence. The Seal of the Prophets, Sayyidina Muhammad 鐃, was the last one who was sent to call people to his caravan, which was the biggest and most important caravan that has moved toward the Divine Presence. And his invitation was international. In every century and among every kind of people who were gathered under the banner of mankind, he was calling to people.

Now, I am saying these words because one of our brothers said to me that some people had asked him to give a talk in a church, and he was asking if he could take the Holy Qur'an in his hand for speaking to people in a church or could bring holy *hadiths* of the Prophet and make a speech for them. Then I said to him, "See if, after a little bit, something comes through our Assembly,[107] and then you may keep it, you may use it."

Anyone may be invited to give a talk about Islam in a church. A church is also built to be a place for worshipping the Lord, Almighty Allah, and Allah Almighty rewards those people according to their intentions. It is impossible for a person not to be rewarded if he has sincere and good intentions. He *must* be rewarded by the Lord, Almighty Allah; don't suppose anything else. A person may be Christian, may be Jewish, may be from another religion, and Allah Almighty looks at his intentions and rewards him.

I heard a tale about a Majusi, a fire-worshipper, who lived in Baghdad. After his death, a grandshaykh looked into Paradise and saw that one there. And he was surprised and asked, "How can you be in Paradise when you were a fire-worshipper?"

Saints have been given divine lights. To true and real believers, Allah Almighty gives through the lights of real faith, and they are from divine lights. But they have been given only to those people who really believe. Therefore, if a person has been given real faith's lights, no distance or dark-

---

[107]That is, through the talk *(sohbet)* during which these words were being spoken.

ness or huge mountains can hold him back; his lights reach everywhere, reaching into your hearts, also. Nothing holds back those lights.

Therefore, that grandshaykh could look into Paradise. (Such people can see Paradise; they have come to be out of time and space, they can look and can see.) And that grandshaykh saw that person, the Majusi, in Paradise and asked, "How can you be here?"

That is in order to give people something of real knowledge and divine knowledge, so that servants may know something about their Lord's attributes and so that no one should be hopeless. Everyone may hope; everyone has a right to be hopeful of his Lord's Mercy Oceans. When Allah Almighty wants to save His servants from the hands of devils, He has endless, countless ways to save them. Therefore, we have rights to be hopeful, fully hopeful.

And when that grandshaykh asked him, the fire-worshipper said, "O my Lord's servant, the reason that I am here in Paradise is a simple, very simple thing. I wasn't taking any care about it, but it happened:

"One day I saw that my child, a little boy, had a piece of bread in his hand, eating it, and I took him by his ear and said, 'Do you not know that this is the holy month for Muslims? They are fasting. Then how are you carrying a piece of bread in your hand and eating it, while people are respecting that this is the holy month? What are you doing?' And I slapped him and took him inside," the Majusi said.

That was the reason why he was in Paradise: first, because he was a Majusi, a fire-worshipper, and he had no responsibility for fasting because he wasn't Muslim, and second, although that was a small boy and there was no fasting for him, even then his father respected Holy Ramadan and taught *adab*, good manners, to his child. Then Allah Almighty was pleased with that servant. When he was ready to leave this life, He sent divine lights, coming on him, and the seed of faith that was planted by Allah Almighty opened, and he said *Shahadah* and entered Paradise.

Therefore, a person may be sincere in his beliefs and have good intentions. And Allah Almighty looks at your heart. If it is correct, all right;

don't be hopeless. And, also, don't be fearless. Hopeless, without hope; fearless, without fear. Yes, you must be fearful, not fearless—fearful of Allah Almighty.

Pharaoh brought more than 250,000 magicians to have a contest with Moses ﷺ. Moses came singly, alone, but they were a very big crowd, and you wouldn't have been able to look at them because they were clothed in such strange and horrible shapes, filling that big plain. And Moses ﷺ came with a big stick, wearing simple clothes and so long a beard.

Then the chief of the magicians came toward Moses ﷺ, standing there. And Moses ﷺ looked at him while he was coming; prophets' eyes see with divine lights. And when that chief magician came, he came surrendered, and he said to Moses ﷺ, "Are you going to begin, or shall we begin the contest?"[108] And it was enough for that person and for that whole huge crowd of magicians to come into Islam, to come into *iman*—only that word.

Allah Almighty was looking at them. What was going to happen, *He* knew. That chief magician, when he came to Moses ﷺ, came humbly and keeping his respect because he was someone who had understanding. When he looked at Moses ﷺ and saw him alone, he knew with exact knowledge that if that person, Moses ﷺ, was the same as ourselves, he would never find the courage to come and compete with our huge crowd here. So Moses' ﷺ authority cannot be coming from the earth; it must be heavenly and therefore I must ask permission. And he came, asking, "Are you going to begin, or do you give us permission to begin?"

That asking permission from Moses ﷺ made Allah Almighty pleased with all those magicians. A magician's work is *kufr*,[109] strongly prohibited. That is the worst job, the worst activity; Allah Almighty never likes it. But when the chief came and asked Moses' permission, that *adab* made Allah Almighty pleased with the whole assembly.

---

[108](7:115, 20:65) The narratives concerning Moses and the magicians are contained in 7:103-126, 10:75-82, 20:57-73 and 26:34-51.

[109]Unbelief, denial of Allah.

Then Moses ﷺ said, "You may begin." And lights, divine lights, came into their hearts, and that seed of belief, the seed of faith, that was planted on the Day of Promises[110] began to grow, quickly growing. And when Moses ﷺ threw down his stick, a huge snake appeared. When it opened its mouth, between its two jaws there was one mile's distance.

Pharaoh was sitting in his palace, and after finishing everything that the magicians had put there, their sticks and ropes, that gigantic snake rushed at Pharaoh, opening its mouth to swallow the whole palace, Allah Almighty bringing him down.

When they saw that happening, all the magicians quickly ran to make *sajdah*, prostrating themselves, and in that *sajdah* Allah Almighty showed each one of them his station in Paradise. And Pharaoh, so angry, said, "What are you doing? You are all partners with this one; Moses is your chief! I shall cut off your hands and feet, and then I shall hang you on the trunks of palm trees!"[111]

And they said, "It doesn't matter; no worry. You can cut, you can do anything to our physical bodies, but our souls are free. We are with our Lord."

Therefore, *adab*, good manners and good behavior, is the fruit of good intentions, always. But good intentions come from sincerity, and sincerity does not come without deep beliefs. And we are asking forgiveness for our bad behavior, bad intentions and bad actions. ▲

---

[110]Referring to: "And when your Lord took from the children of Adam, from their loins, their descendants and made them testify concerning themselves, [saying to them], "Am I not your Lord?" They said, "Yes, we have testified [to it]," lest you should say on the Day of Resurrection, "Indeed, we were unaware of this" (7:172)

[111]The story of the repentance of the magicians is told in 7:123-126, 20:71-73 and 26:49-51.

25: CARRYING life's BURDens with patience

Every building needs a base; every structure stands upon a base, yes? This building, without a base, a foundation, would never stand up, and a strong building must have a strong foundation.

There is a big mosque in Istanbul, one of the biggest mosques in the Islamic world, Sulemaniye. This night it is going to be full, about 50,000 people entering it for the Night of Power; tonight we are observing it. And this famous mosque has a story.

Süleyman, Sultan Sulaiman the Magnificent, ordered his architect to build for him a mosque, a big mosque, to be magnificent. As the *sultan* was magnificent, so must his mosque also be magnificent. And, as he had been ordered, the architect made foundations, and a foundation means digging with pickaxe and shovel—not these machines, coming and doing it quickly, no. They went down to the depth where water comes; down to there they dug. When the water came, it was enough digging, and he filled up the whole foundation.

Then he disappeared. And the *sultan* was very angry and ordered all the people of the empire to try to find that person. "Quickly bring him to me!"

One year, two years, three years, four years. "Where is this person? I am going to die and this person has disappeared! If he is not going to build it, we must look for another one. But he was the magnificent one, also, in his architecture."

Yes. Then, when it was going to be seven years, that architect reappeared. The *sultan* was too angry. "Where were you?!!!"

"O *Sultan*, you are the *sultan*! You know what you are doing. But you are not an architect. The architect *I* am. You understand about governing this empire, but this building *I* understand. You do not understand. If I had not disappeared and had built as you ordered, quickly, then perhaps after one year or ten years this would have fallen down.

"Now I will build a building and will put on it such a dome that, if, on the Last Day, there is an earthquake throughout the whole world, this dome will fall down and roll like a helmet on the ground, not breaking. I am that architect; you are the *sultan*. This building *I* have responsibility for."

We are saying this for understanding that every important building must be built on strong foundations. Then, what about Islam, which we know from the Prophet 🌺?

Our teachers have taught us that Islam has how many "pillars"? Five pillars. But these pillars must be raised on a strong foundation. And what is that foundation?

The Prophet 🌺 said, *"Utitu jawam'i-l-kalim.*[112] I have been given authority to speak, and if I say a few words, they may contain an ocean of knowledge." And his inheritors, *awliya*, also have such an authority to speak or to give an understanding, to give wisdoms, in brief words.

Grandshaykh was one of those inheritors, no doubt, and he was saying, "O Nazim Efendi, the foundation that Islam is raised on is one thing. It is also so for every religion, because Islam is the universal, original religion from the beginning, from the time of Adam up to the end. And Islam is just built on one thing, and that is *tahammul*—to be able to carry or to bear everything that may come to the children of Adam."

In this life everything is just loaded upon the children of Adam. This life is a heavy burden on everyone, and you have been ordered to carry that heavy burden. Therefore, Islam and its pillars are trusts from Allah Almighty, and you have been ordered to carry those trusts on your shoulders.

---

[112]"I have been given conciseness [or comprehensiveness] of speech."

When Allah Almighty called the mountains and all the seven worlds and the seven heavens, and ordered them to carry His divine trust, *amanah*, they said, "O our Lord, are You ordering us to carry that or giving a choice to us? We are saying, 'We can't. Forgive us. We can't carry that.'"[113] Then Allah Almighty made it like a piece of stone and Adam lifted it a little bit, and—like this, like this, like this—lifted it higher and higher. When he had raised it to his middle, Allah Almighty said, "It is going to be on your shoulders, My divine trust. *You* should carry it."

"Innahu kana dhaluman jahula"[114]—man is too *dhalim*, unjust and cruel, in not looking after that divine trust, to keep it; Allah knows that they are unjust and ignorant about their Lord's rights. And we are carrying it; all the children of Adam, we are carrying that divine trust, or we have been asked to carry it. And you can't carry it if you haven't any belief in your Lord; if you are not a believer you can't carry that divine trust.

Every divine command that has come through prophets to ourselves is a heavy burden, but without being able to carry that heavy burden, it is impossible to keep those divine commands. Therefore, our religion, Islam, and all the religions which are Islam, also,[115] are just built on being able to carry everything. In other words, when the Prophet was asked, *"Ma al-iman*—what is *iman*, what is faith?" he replied only with one word, saying, *"As-sabr*, to be patient."

"To be patient" means to be able to carry every heavy burden on your shoulders; that is being patient. Now, we are saying this, and our grand-shaykh, Abu Yazid [al-Bistami], was also saying, "The meaning of *tariqat*, in our view, is to be able to carry every unliked thing during your life; that is the meaning of *tariqat* that I am giving to you. If anyone is asking what is the meaning of *tariqat*, I am saying to him, 'To be able to carry every burden

---

[113]Referring to: "Indeed, We offered the Trust [of obligations and obedience to Allah] to the heavens and earth and the mountains, and they declined to bear it and feared it." (33:72)

[114]"Indeed, he [man] was unjust and ignorant" (33:72), the continuation of the verse cited in footnote 113.

[115]Meaning that what was revealed to all the true prophets prior to Muhammad ﷺ was also Islam.

during this life.'" And it means to be sufficiently powerful in one's faith, because if a person is not powerful enough in his beliefs, he can't carry those difficult burdens.

Who can carry heavy burdens? Only those people who believe in their Lord's rewards and prizes, because He says, *"Innama yuwaffa-s-sabiruna ajra-hum bi-ghairi hisab"*;[116] Allah Almighty promising that those people who are carrying every heavy burden during their lives should be given prizes and rewarded with endless divine favors and endless mercies. Whoever believes in that may carry, may be patient. If not, it is as though you are asking a person to do a heavy piece of work and he says, "I can't do it." You say, "I shall give you ten pounds." He says, "No." "I will give you twenty." He says, "No." "I will give you fifty pounds." He says, "No." "I will give you one hundred pounds." He says, "I can't." "I will give you one thousand." Then he is going to shake and tremble. "You are really going to give me one thousand?" You say, "Yes, I shall give it to you." You give it to him and then he can do that difficult work.

Yes, as much as servants are carrying heavy burdens, they will be given more rewards. Therefore, you must believe in your Lord, Allah Almighty's, saying, "I will pay you endlessly. There will be eternal, never-ending favors for you if you are patient." Whoever believes in that may be patient.

Therefore, you can see believers being patient, but unbelievers can't be patient—never. If people were patient, there would be no more hospitals, no more prisons, no more courts. But when beliefs go down, people become impatient.

One of our sisters was asking and expressing a kind of complaint that from every side are coming thorns: from children, from husband, from neighbors, from our community, also, and she was becoming upset. And there is no cure except to believe in our Lord, Allah Almighty. He never leaves His servants during this life without a trial, and He is asking His servants only to be patient.

---

[116]should read: See footnote 62.

Yes, you must be patient, everyone, as much as you can. And that grandshaykh, Sultan al-'Arifin Abu Yazid, was saying and was practicing, also, his words. He was saying, "I kept myself amongst my family in my house and I tested myself to see if I was patient with my family, most of all with my wife."

That is important for a man, to be able to carry his wife. First you must be with her, bearing, carrying her, and then you must carry children, little ones—crying, shouting, breaking things. For everything you see, you must be patient.

He was testing himself—one day, two days, one week, two weeks. And then he was saying, "Now I am all right with my family. I know that they are parts of myself and I am carrying them. But it is not enough. I must also carry other people." And he was going out, going through the markets, among people, and testing himself to see whether he could carry people, also.

Yes, it is important also to carry people. All the prophets carried them. For some of them, there were so many people harming them, and then finally the prophets made *du'a*, supplication, against them. Noah, for nine hundred-and-fifty years, carried his nation. Each day he went out and called people to his Lord's worship, and they were throwing on him stones and sticks, making him fall down and then leaving him. They would say, "He is dead now," and go.

For 950 years he bore it. Then he said, *"Rabbi, la tadhar 'ala-l-ardi mina-l-kafirina dayyara,"*[117] and Allah Almighty sent the Flood. But our Prophet ﷺ said, "I was the one who bore people's *adhah*, harm, the most. No one bore as much as I bore." Allah Almighty's order is to bear, to carry, and the *sunnah* of our Prophet, for his nation, is to bear.

We are gathered and living here for this holy month, and we must be patient for carrying each other, and also we must be careful that we do not harm anyone. Trials from Allah Almighty are going on; sometimes, without

---

[117]"My Lord, do not leave a single one of the unbelievers upon the earth." (71:26)

our will, comes some un-liked thing. We must be patient, we must carry it. As much as you can carry trials, you are going to develop your faith and you should find more spiritual improvement. Whoever is able to be more patient, he improves in his spiritual development.

Therefore, Abu Yazid was going around his town, his city, to see if he was able to carry people. He tested himself for a while and then he said, "O my ego, you are a well-known person in your city. Everyone knows you and respects you. You must go to some foreign countries where they do not know you and may harm you with their actions, with their words. You must go. I am not trusting that you are carrying everyone."

And he went and traveled around various countries and saw whether he could carry people or not. Then he gave a sign that it was all right. "I can trust you, O my ego, that you are carrying everyone." And that is the top point of faith, to be patient enough to carry people, because every prophet carried them, and our beloved Muhammad ﷺ just bore every harm from people. Therefore, you can't find anyone who has improved in his faith without bearing people and their harm.

And we are in need of this, particularly in our time when people are getting more egotistical, when they only like their egos and are less respectful to one another, because day by day they are weaker in their beliefs, and if no belief, then no respect among people. People are becoming like robots, only sharing in benefits; they are looking and coming together for the purpose of investment only, nothing else, to get some advantage. If that goes on among them, no one will bring them together, and their love also is not coming from heart to heart; finished. No more real love among people now because they are not giving *heart* love; they are giving another kind of "love," not heart love.

I saw a couple and they were saying, "We have been together for fifty years," an English family. But everyone whom I ask, "Are you married?" is saying, "Once I was"—*everyone!* Those people are very few now; to continue for fifty years means that they are giving their love from heart to heart. But others are not giving their love; it is 'love' as cats in March give 'love' to each other—you know?—and afterwards, no more love among cats.

Now civilization is like cats' civilization, cats' love—for three days, three months or six months; then finished. *That is love?* Therefore, it has no reality; neither one can carry the other. Real faith makes people carry each other, and if a wife is not able to carry her husband or if a husband is not able to carry his wife, who can carry another person? No one! And that is the cause of illness, those crises which are increasing in our time in every branch of our life. And the way is only to believe with real faith and to be sincere with your Lord, and your Lord will support you for every burden and will support you to carry His divine trust. ▲

26: the importance of beliefs

Association with a shaykh gives more power to our faith, and then it gives familiarity to everyone who attends such an assembly and meeting. But the characteristic of our egos is never to be familiar with anyone. Every ego wants to be independent, by itself. It should be the first and only one among people, as a king is never going to agree to let someone sit on the same throne with himself.

That is the characteristic of our egos, always wanting to be the only one in its stage or in its station. The people of Pharaoh, the Egyptian ruler, were a nation worshipping idols; so many idols, so many gods or goddesses, they worshipped. But Pharaoh didn't agree to be one among all these. He wanted to be the chief, the head one. *"Fa-qala, 'Ana Rabbukumu-l-A'la,"*[118] he claimed. "O people, I am your most famous, most honored Lord. The most important one, that is *I.*"

And each one among mankind has an ego; you can't find anyone without an ego. Everyone has been given an ego, and ego has the same attribute from beginning to end. Its characteristic never changes.

On the Night Journey, Allah Almighty addressed His Holy Prophet, beloved Muhammad 🌸, and said, "O My servant, beloved Muhammad, if I were to give such an opportunity or chance as I gave to Pharaoh, each one of My servants would be just like Pharaoh. They would say to people, 'I am your greatest Lord.' If they find the same conditions and same power and authority that I gave to Pharaoh, they are going to be like him."

---

[118]"Then he [Pharaoh] said, 'I am your most exalted Lord.'" (79:24)

Therefore, you must be careful about your ego and you must not blame anyone, even Pharaoh. Don't say that Pharaoh was such a bad one. You can't believe in *your* ego, either, because Allah Almighty is saying, "If I leave you free and no one is commanding you, you are going to be like Pharaoh. You will also say, 'I am your Lord,' to people. But I am not giving that chance to you." Therefore, you must look at your own ego and don't blame anyone because he does not worship or he is not a good-charactered person. If we are left in the hands of our egos, our ways will also go in that direction.

Therefore, this assembly gives familiarity to the attenders because if any group meets for the sake of Allah, for the love of our Lord, then the Lord, Almighty Allah, sends upon the attenders from His divine Mercy Oceans, covering them. It is such an effective mercy that if even one drop comes on a person—even if he is an unbeliever, only coming to see what those people are, what they are doing, out of curiosity coming and looking from the door to see who is there, those people sitting, and little by little coming and sitting down, curious—if that drop from divine Mercy Oceans falls on him, coming on his soul, even if he leaves this meeting and never returns, that is going to affect that person's inner life.

As an example, I may say that there is a bad illness now, very bad and dangerous; no one can be saved if that comes to a person. From very simple things it may come to people, and it is impossible to be saved from it. I am using an example from that bad thing, and also from Allah Almighty, because we are sitting here for the sake of our Lord and we are sitting in His love.

We are not sitting here for the enjoyment of this life. Whoever wants enjoyment and pleasure for this life, outside there is too much; he can go. No one is coming here asking for his physical body's pleasure, but our souls are thirsty for those Mercy Oceans and then we are attending here, and most people are coming from the far East, from the far West, from far countries. They are not coming here for eating or drinking—they can find eating and drinking in their own countries, also—but the thing which is gathering people in this place is only the love that Allah Almighty puts into each heart. But most people are imprisoning that love in a deep part of their hearts; they are not opening the door for it to come out.

And therefore we are here in the love of our Lord, attending, and that Mercy Ocean comes, and if even one drop comes on a person, it is a sign that that person is going to be a happy one. Finally he should come to the caravan that is moving toward Allah Almighty's Divine Presence.

Yes. Two caravans are moving, and everyone must join one of these two caravans. One caravan is the prophets' caravan and saints' caravan and believers' caravan, and the other one, the second caravan, is the Devil's caravan, Satan's caravan, the Anti-Christ's caravan. Everyone may choose one of these two for himself. The prophets' caravan is calling to people, "O people! We are moving to our Lord's Divine Presence. You have an invitation from your Lord. Come along and join us!"

At first, perhaps it is difficult for your egos because we are passing through huge deserts, difficult mountains and terrible valleys, but at the end we will reach a plain where you may enjoy yourself up to eternity. But the second caravan has too many advertisers, calling people—too many: "O people! Come and join our caravan. It is a free caravan. Come and join and enjoy yourselves, people!"

And people are dancing, running—yes! But as at first a student, if he can be patient and carry so much studying, keeps himself away from every-thing else and sits and learns, at the end he is going to be so pleased and to enjoy himself. But the one who is always playing, running from this way, from that way, at the end of the year he must cry—yes!

Therefore, we are living in a world in which all things are going to be a test for everyone. The prophets are saying, "If you join our caravan, at the end you will take your rest, you will find peace, you will find every enjoy-ment. Don't be cheated or deceived by devils. They are saying, 'Come and drink! Come and eat! Come and enjoy yourself!' But at the end, finally, too much crying, too much regret."

But your egos, like little boys, may run and ask for everything, whether harmful or harmless, running after it, and they are mostly listening to the caravan of devils and Satan, and asking to follow them. But each time our ego follows them, there comes regret. *Must be!*

Yes. We are living in a life which we are able to keep for only the moment we are in. Every breath which we leave behind ourselves and everything which is ahead of us, after a second, it is also going to be behind us. As a car runs speedily and swallows the road, quickly for us, also, every breath is just finishing our lives. We can't keep past time with ourselves; past time is finished. And we are waiting for the future, but the future also quickly comes and runs from our hands. Therefore, every enjoyment in this life is like a dream, and from a dream no one can take anything. You may see, you may dream, that you are sitting on a throne with a crown on your head and with treasures, but you can't keep that. When you open your eyes, nothing, and you are saying, "Where did they go? They were with me just now."

Yes. Therefore, our egos are always cheating us, and we must be serious about our temporary life. We must look after it seriously because during our temporary life we can take only spiritual development and improvement, and no one can improve or develop without joining the caravan of prophets and saints. *That must be.*

Now, there is an important point to say to you. In Western countries I am seeing or I am meeting a lot of people, and they are claiming that they have wisdoms—from this, from that. They are reading books or listening and learning and keeping with themselves wisdoms from the East, from oriental countries.

Oriental countries are a dream for European people particularly, as oriental people are also always dreaming of these Western countries—yes, too happy to come to London, to England, to live in Germany, dreaming people. And whoever dreams of Western countries, *ghusl*, showering, is *wajib*, necessary, for him.[119]

---

[119]In Islam, *ghusl* or showering is the means of cleaning from major impurity. The meaning here is that an equal degree of spiritual impurity is incurred when people from the spiritually luminous East dream about the spiritually darker Western world.

Whenever European, Western, people think about oriental countries, countries of the sunrise, refreshment comes into their hearts, spiritual refreshment and light, but whenever oriental countries' people think about the countries of the sunset, Western countries, darkness comes into their hearts. That is a bad thing, because their hearts are looking to that eastward direction; no good. And whoever comes here, if they feel light in their own countries, when they come here, darkness comes—if not the darkness of night, at least the darkness of a cloudy sky.[120]

And you are asking for wisdoms from Eastern countries because all prophets and all prophethood has come from the Middle East, from oriental countries, and wisdoms have come from those countries, also. Even old Greek wisdoms have taken their lights from the East; they never looked to the West but always to the East. Now, I mean to say that so many Western people want wisdoms and are suffering to reach some wisdoms, even on the plains of India or in Tibet, and they have brought some wisdoms. Then what is the difficulty for them?

The difficulty is that they are bringing wisdoms like beads, so many, like beads, they are carrying and bringing. But if a lady has a pearl necklace, does she carry the pearls in her hand or put them on a silk thread?

She puts them on a strong thread, to keep them; otherwise they are going to be lost. Therefore, although people are taking so many wisdoms, and they are sufficiently proud of their wisdoms, finally they are losing them because there is not a strong thread keeping them.

What is that thread? I must say it now. What is this thread for those pearls? Wisdom's pearls should be kept, but with which thing can you keep them?

---

[120]Shaykh Nazim adds parenthetically: Therefore, if the [British] government heard me, it would give me a medal because I am saying, "Oriental people, leave these countries and go back to your own countries," but no one is saying to Mrs. Thatcher or to Her Majesty the Queen that I am such a person, advising your foreigners here to go back to their sun-shining, oriental countries that you are dreaming about—yes!

With a strong belief; *strong belief keeps wisdoms.* Without believing in any religion, finished; they are going to be lost. Therefore, as a person likes, he must follow either Christianity or Judaism or Islam. He must keep *one* belief; otherwise everything that he has gained is going to be useless. And that is something that people who are asking for wisdoms from the East, from the West, are forgetting, and it is the most important thing. If you have this, then, one after the other, you can take pearls, but if you haven't got this, then everything that you are taking of wisdoms is going to be lost.

Therefore, you must believe in a religion. I am not saying to you that you must believe in this one or that one or that one, but you must not do it by taking something from Christianity, something from Judaism, something from Islam. It is nonsense, without meaning—*without meaning, because beliefs need to be pure.* If beliefs are not pure, they are going to be mixed-up and are going to be useless.

Therefore, you may try to believe in some belief and you must not be cheated by titles. You must look at meanings and purposes and principles. If the principles are correct, you may keep it, and when you accept the principles of a belief, you must try to keep to your belief, just as, if you have a pearl necklace, you must look after it carefully because thieves may steal it. Therefore, beliefs must also be protected, and you must know which things protect your belief. If not protecting it, you will not be able to find it, also; it will be stolen. And if anyone makes up something, makes up a religion by himself, it is going to be wrong.

Therefore, we must follow heavenly religions and heavenly beliefs, and we are believing as our Lord is asking us to believe. Every heavenly religion—Christianity, also, and Islam and Judaism—is calling people to believe in the existence of the Lord, Almighty God, and in His unity, and then calling people to believe in the Last Day, Judgment Day. Without believing in Judgment Day there is no religion. It is useless, because religion gives responsibility to mankind.

We are human beings, we are not animals. Animals do not carry responsibility, but we are from mankind. You have been honored and, as you have been honored, you have been loaded with responsibility. Therefore, that is among the most important pillars of religion.

The most, *most* important, is to believe in the existence of the Lord, the Creator, and His unity, and second, to believe that He has a judgment day for His servants. You must understand that you have responsibility for the Day of Resurrection and that you will be judged that Day, and you must believe in the eternal life either in Paradise or in Hells. That is a never-changing belief.

If anyone believes in these, the wisdom-pearls that he takes will give him benefit because wisdoms make or keep people in humanity, keeping people honored, keeping people honorable. The one who has wisdoms is never going to be a dishonorable person. If a person has wisdoms he can't be a liar, if a person has been given wisdoms he is not going to be cruel, and so on. Wisdoms give people honor, and those wisdoms, when you believe in Judgment Day, give you more power during your life, giving you a direction toward your destination—your true destination, not the wrong destination, never leaving you to follow devils or to fall into evils, no. ▲

27: fighting your ego and being with truth

What is honor for a person? Honor and being honorable is to accept truth; that is honor for people, for everyone. Whoever accepts truth, he has been honored by accepting it. And which thing makes a person dishonorable? To reject truth, while truth is always like the sun in the skies.

Truth is not hidden; always it is clear. And do you think that Abu Jahl, the biggest enemy to the Prophet,[121] didn't know the truth? His conscience proclaimed the truth, proclaimed that Muhammad ﷺ had brought the truth, the absolute truth, the unquestionable truth, but his ego came and prevented him.

In his conscience everyone knows what is truth but his ego rejects it. Therefore, ego is cursed because it prevents people from accepting truth. It is only our ego, *nafs*, which makes people dishonorable, and therefore Allah Almighty orders His servants to fight their egoes. And the Prophet was saying, *"Umirtu an uqatila-n-nasa hatta yaqulu 'La ilaha illa-Llah.'"*[122]

You must understand what is the main or the last message of beloved Muhammad ﷺ; you must look at what he brought, for what he struggled, for which thing he gave his life, his whole life. You must not be fanatical or egotistical, and fanatical people are egotistical people. You must accept what is truth. And he, the Prophet ﷺ, was summarizing his prophethood and saying, "I have been ordered to struggle with people until they accept to say '*La ilaha illa-Llah*, there is no God but Allah.'"

---

[121]One of the Prophet's uncles and most bitter opponents.

[122]"I have been ordered to struggle with people until they say, 'There is no deity except Allah.'"

We are saying, claiming that we are the followers of the *Sunnah* of the Prophet, *Ahlu's-Sunnah*.[123] And so many people in our time are claiming that they are keeping only the *Sunnah*, but their egos are raising themselves over them and putting reins in their mouths, making them like donkeys.

What is the reason? The main *sunnah*, the most famous *sunnah*, is the Prophet's saying, "I have been ordered to oppose people until they accept to say that there is no God but Allah."[124] And you, each one, as a follower of our beloved Prophet ﷺ, you must keep a staff for fighting; you must keep a staff in your hand to fight until your ego says "There is no God but Allah," because your ego, or every ego, says, "There is no God but Me, only *Me*." Therefore Shaykh Hasan is saying in his song, "Me-Me-Me, Me-Me-Me!" You must listen to that song.

Your ego is saying to you, "You must not accept any God except Me, and I am your Lord," because it will never be able to command anyone except you. "You must be an obedient servant to *Me* only, and I am your Lord. You must accept Me as your Lord!" And you are saying, "O my Lord, yes, sir! Whatever you order, I am ready."

Everyone—that is our characteristic! Therefore, you must accept truth. If you say, "My ego is an angel," you are a liar. Your ego is not an angel and it is never going to be at the level of an angel. Instead, you can say, "It is a devil, a real devil." More than Satan it is a devil, our ego; you must be very careful. Therefore, the Prophet said, "*'Ada-l-'adu nafsuka-l-lati baina jambaik*,[125] the most terrible and dangerous devil is in the middle of your chest, here."

---

[123] People of the Prophet's *Sunnah*.

[124] This is a continuation of the thought that was expressed on page 108. The meaning here is that the Lord of creation commanded His Prophet ﷺ to fight the Arabian polytheists who denied His right to be obeyed and worshipped by ascribing divinity and authority to fictitious entities other than Him. It should be noted that these polytheists never thought of denying the existence of the Creator but rather that they ascribed divine attributes to idols or other imaginary deities. This is clear from the multiple references to the pagans' acknowledging and invoking Allah and ar-Rahman as the Creator, as mentioned in such verses as 6:23, 10:31, 17:110, 19:88, 21:26, 23:84-89, 36:15, 39:38, 43:20.

[125] "The worst of enemies is your *nafs* which is between your two sides."

All prophets came with truth but the *whole* truth is in the widsoms of Muhammad 🌸, and you must accept this. If you do not accept it, you will never reach the level of humanity and you are not going to be an honorable person in the Divine Presence. Therefore, we must fight our ego and say, "Get away! I am now with truth."

Your ego makes one thousand or one hundred thousand traps or tricks for you, for changing your mind, and for changing your heart, also. Don't suppose that it is an easy one to fight—no! Instead, it is so difficult. You may fight everyone on earth and they may be easy in comparison to your ego, it is so difficult.

How is it not going to be difficult when the Prophet 🌸 says that it is the biggest enemy, the biggest devil? Yet you are looking after it so carefully; you are using every means to make your ego pleased, to give it pleasure. Who can say, "I am not trying to make my ego at rest and in pleasure and enjoyment?" Everyone does! And every problem and every crisis and wars, all fighting, every bad thing, grows from that point: that everyone wants to make his ego in the most excellent condition and best enjoyment, to give it everything that it may ask.

This world is not enough for the ego of a person. If anyone is given this world, he will ask for another one. But leave aside the whole world. If you give him this London, taking all the people out of it and giving it to him, by nighttime he will go to the mental hospital; he will be crazy because he will go around, like this, like that—no one in an empty city, a dead city, a ghost town. Yes, he will go, he will run, through the streets and roads, and from here up to there, looking to see if someone is there.

Now we have given you this London. Take it; we will go away to another London. But he does not want to be alone; he wants the whole of London to be for himself and also for all the people to be under his command. Ego is not happy by itself only, no. But if I were able, I would imprison it in an empty town, a ghost town, to have ghosts looking at it from every side, also.

Devils, our egos! Therefore, it is so difficult a one to fight. But until you are going to be victorious over it, you can't be a person who accepts truth, no; it makes you dishonorable, always. When your ego says, "Now I am surrendering. As you say, I am proclaiming that there is no God but Allah," *then* you will be honored here and Hereafter.

In our time a lot of people are claiming that they are asking for truth, that they are looking for truth. But what is the benefit if truth shines like a sun but still you are denying it, you are not proclaiming it? And do you think that as long as you are under your ego's control you will accept truth? No!

We have now in our time, also, truth. Islam just brought truth, absolute truth; you can't find anything in Islam except truth. Never can anyone object to the principles that Islam brought as beliefs, as worships, as attributes of character; no one can make any objection.

And if people are making objections about what Islam fought against, Islam just fought against devils. For what did prophets come if people, all of them, accepted truth? And the Last Prophet 襲 was sent as a prophet when his nation was in the midst of the darkness of ignorance. In too heavy darkness they were; they were in the worst condition through *dhulm*, cruelty. Who can imagine a tribe of people who buried innocent girls under the sun?[126] Which community has done such cruelty? It means their hearts were like rocks. And yet some no-mind people are defending them!

For what did Muhammad 襲 struggle? He had to oppose those people; they were devils, representing and practicing the rules of devils. If you did not struggle against them, you would have to give them your neck, for them to cut it off. But so many foolish and fanatical people—in our time, also, so many—are making objections about why Islam struggled.

How was he *not* going to struggle? He came as a prophet, with truth, and they were objecting and refusing truth, insisting that they could do anything they liked of cruelty and that no one should say "No" to them. Why do these governments make prisons and punish people? Leave them, in their freedom; they can do anything if that is true! But anyone who fights

---

[126]In the Arabian society of the Prophet's time, girls were often buried alive during infancy or childhood.

the government, the government must fight him. That is a rule, never changing.

Therefore, Islam is perfect in every direction; no one can make any objection to Islam, can say that there is anything imperfect in Islam. That is truth. You may hate the name of Islam or Muslims but you must not hate truth. Anyone who wants to be honored here and Hereafter must proclaim truth, and truth is equal to Islam and Islam is equal to truth. People are asking for some way to practice, but I have never seen a way better than Islam for practicing, for beliefs and worships and character. You *must* accept!

Therefore, we have been ordered to fight our egos until they say that Islam is the perfect religion from every direction. In beliefs and worships and dealing with people, they can never find anything better than the *Shari'ah's* rules for governing people. Every day people are making a new rule, the next day saying, "This is not good, we must change it." Every government is like this, full-up with rules, and every parliament is coming and making new ones. "This is no good. Bring something else!" and writing new ones.

Allah sent His rule which is suitable for individuals and collectively. Why are you are rejecting it? I am shouting this because Allah, the Almighty Lord, is pleased with me when I am shouting at people. [Laughter.] I am the defender of the holy rules (If anyone is objecting, I will send to him one ghost, entering at nighttime!)

Yes. So many secret powers have not yet appeared. Don't think that you know everything or that every power is under your control. There are certain ones controlling all the power that you are so proud of and, only with a switch, a key, turning it back, finishing off everything, and you will see what is the power of faith. It is soon coming because this world is soon going to be uncontrolled by anyone. Yet there are certain ones controlling everything. Don't think that those reactors or clouds [Chernobyl] are going like this, coming like that, without control. There are commanders for the winds, also; yes.

Truth is sweet, but some people, ill people, when you give them sweet things, are saying, "Bitter, bitter, bitter!" I am giving this sweet thing and he is saying, "Bitter," giving this bitter one and he is saying, "Sweet." It means, finished; no more life for that person. Therefore *haqq*, truth, is sweet and beautiful, and we must accept it.

We have just arrived at the last Friday of this holy month, and it has passed so quickly. And everything that is numbered must be finished. If it is not just one month but one year, it is still going to finish quickly.

Everything that is temporary one day is going to be finished. What is permanent, *that* is important, and we are coming to this life to gain permanent life, permanent pleasure, and to make our Lord pleased with ourselves. When we make our Lord pleased with ourselves, then *that* is going to be pleasure, here and Hereafter.

We are believers. This is a holy month. The Prophet ﷺ was giving good tidings about this holy month. The first one-third of this Holy Ramadan is the days of mercy, coming on all people, ten days, and the second ten days are the days of forgiveness of our Lord, Almighty Allah. And the last one-third, which we are going to finish now, also, is freedom from Hells for believers, Allah Almighty making them free, keeping them away from Hells. Therefore, believers who are trying to keep our Lord's orders during the days of Holy Ramadan by fasting and during the night by praying *Tarawih*[127] and other prayers, may be rewarded by our Lord, Almighty Allah, giving them *bara'at*, immunity, safety, from Hells, and they have been given good tidings of Paradise.

And we are the nation of the Last Prophet. One hundred and twenty-four thousand prophets and their nations have passed away. And the Seal of the Prophets, who was the last—no more prophethood or no more prophets after beloved Muhammad ﷺ—was informing people and saying that when I am sent with the last message from my Lord, between me and the Last Day, the Day of Judgment, there is only these two fingers' distance

---

[127]The special nightly prayers of Ramadan.

(and he was making a sign with his two fingers, the middle finger and the *Shahadah*, first, finger), it is so near.

And now, from that time up to today, fifteen centuries have passed, and for everything that we are seeing—because he informed us of every event or every sign before the Last Day comes—he spoke about those signs. He informed us about the conditions that would come and that people would be in when the Last Day approaches; he informed us about difficulties, general difficulties for all people, but particularly for believers.

The Prophet ﷺ was saying that when the Last Day approaches, there will be difficult conditions, and the hearts of believers are going to be melted as salt melts in water because they will see so many bad things, and the whole world will be full-up with evils. There will be the sovereignty of devils on all the world, and believers will see that but they will never be able to change those bad conditions.

No one among believers can accept or agree with such conditions that people now are living in, but you can't do anything. You can't do, you can't say, anything for your children; you can't do anything for your neighbors; you can't do anything for your nation. A day ago a newspaper wrote that in a Muslim country, one person only said the word *"Shari'ah"* and the government took that the person to prison—a person only mentioning *Shari'ah*, when that country carried the flag of the Prophet for six hundred years! Yes, how changed—changed, because the time is approaching, and believers' hearts are melting, but we, you, can't do anything.

And then the *sahabah*, the Prophet's Companions, were asking him, "O Prophet, how can believers live among such difficult conditions? How will their lives be? Is it possible to live under such conditions?"

And the Prophet ﷺ said, "As bacteria live in vinegar, so they will live." And you must be patient, and you must ask from your Lord, Allah Almighty.

The Children of Israel were asking their Lord to send them a holy man who was supported by divine powers to fight against unbelievers.[128] But we are heedless people, the whole Islamic world; we are *not* asking that.

Even though the Prophet gave good tidings about that one, that holy one who will be supported by divine powers and divine attributes,[129] giving good tidings for the nation of Muhammad ﷺ, yet so many scholars are denying him and making discussions: "Is such a person coming or not coming?" But even if he were not mentioned in *hadiths*, so many *hadiths*, still we must ask for him because Allah Almighty can do anything, and we may ask Him to give us such a holy man, holy person, supported by divine powers, to stop every evil and to defeat every devil.

And you must ask! It is obligatory for every believer to ask from Allah Almighty, "O my Lord! O Allah, *ya Rabb*! Send us someone to save the nation of Muhammad ﷺ." And it is enough for everyone to look after himself and to ask from his Lord divine support, individually and generally, for all people. We are asking not only for believers but we are asking for all nations to be safe from the hands of devils. ▲

---

[128]Referring to 2:246: "Have you not considered the assembly of the Children of Israel after [the time of] Moses, when they said to a prophet of theirs [Saul], "Send to us a king, and we will fight in the way of Allah"?

[129]That is, Sayyidina al-Mahdi ؏.

28: understanding the purpose of our lives

The holy month has quickly passed away, taking something from ourselves, also, like a plane coming from the Heavens, landing on earth and then taking away something. Whoever has given something, it is put there and taken to the Divine Presence. And we hope that Allah Almighty forgives us and gives to us from His endless Mercy Oceans.

O believers, we believe in the life hereafter. And whoever believes in the life hereafter, the eternal life, he must know about his position during this life and he must have an aim for his life.

The Prophet ﷺ said, *"Al-hikmata-d-dallata-l-mu'min. 'Indama wajadaha an takhadhaha."*[130] Wisdoms are all the property of Muslims but they are lost property. Therefore, anywhere they can find a wisdom, they may take it and say, "This belongs to us. I had lost it but now I have found it."

No fanatacism in Islam, particularly no fanatacism for knowledge. That *hadith*, that saying from the Prophet ﷺ, gives a wide horizon to believers. If they can find a wisdom in India, they may take it, as the Prophet said, *"Utlubu-l-'ilma wa law bis-Sin*[131]— if you can find a wisdom in China (at that time it was known as the farthest country), you may go and take it."

If a person brings you wisdoms, you may take them. But now in our time, even among ourselves, we are making so much trouble about taking some wisdoms, even from Muslims who are well-known as good persons, great people in Islam, making so much criticism.

---

[130]"Wisdom is the lost property of the believer. Wherever he finds it, he may take it."
[131]Literally, "Seek knowledge, even though it be in China."

Now I will say one word about such wisdoms. Islam just came among an ignorant tribe, the Quraysh, the people of *jahiliyyah*,[132] and the Prophet 🕊, by the holy command of his Lord, Allah Almighty, brought the Last Message. He had 124,000 *sahabah*, Companions, taking them from *asfala safilin*,[133] the lowest degree (perhaps lower than the level of animals because you can't see an animal that will kill its child, and at that time they were killing their children, burying them alive), and changing them from *asfal*, the lowest, to the highest horizon of humanity.

This point must be well-known, how the Prophet and how Islam affect people. And Islam is so *walud*,[134] giving more and more at every time. We are not like a religion in which only a few people are appearing as scholars, *'ulama*, or as *awliya*, no; at every time you can find thousands and thousands of people who are reaching the horizon of humanity. No objection; we can be happy and peaceful that there are such people in Islam at every time.

We are now speaking about a wisdom, and it is going to give us an understanding of our goal. Ibrahim Adham was one of the famous personalities of Islam, well-known in the East and in the West, also. He was a *sultan* in his time, and Allah Almighty gave everything to him and he had every means to enjoy with his ego.

One of his enjoyments was hunting. Hunting is also something useful; for *jihad*, warfare, and for our bodies it is good. He was hunting one day, chasing a deer. Then from his saddle a voice, *hatif*, came to him, saying, "*Ya Ibrahim, a-li hadha khuliqta aw li hadha umirt?*"[135]

He listened. What was the meaning? "O Sultan Ibrahim, do you think that you have been created for this purpose? Do you suppose that you

---

[132]Ignorance; specifically, of the divine guidance.
[133]"The lowest of the low." (95:5)
[134]Fertile, productive, fruitful.
[135]"O Abraham, have you been created for this or have you been ordered to do this?"

have been created and ordered to do this?" And he was shocked, not see-ing anyone speaking to him but hearing that voice.

That is suitable for the holy command of Allah, showing people for what purpose they have been created, asking him, "Were you created for hunting, for enjoying yourself always, or is this the holy command for eve-ryone—to enjoy themselves in this life with hunting, with playing?" And no answer.

That question is for all of us, for everyone. Each one will be asked it in the Divine Presence when he looks at his life-story. In a second's time you will look at your life-story, the Prophet saying that seventy 'cassettes,' tapes, are recording our lives; seventy records, each one going up to the horizon, extending as far as your vision can reach—seventy for everyone, to see his own life-story.

Now some people are putting on television a half-hour for that per-son, for this person, their life-stories. But that is nothing. You will see sev-enty there, but in one second's time you will be able to look at all of them, not seeing them one by one; everything will happen in one second, in a moment, quickly. And then Allah Almighty will ask, "O My servant, did I create you for such a life? Did I order you to live such a life?" Yes, you must look to your answer.

I am saying this to my self, to my *nafs*, also. If you are listening, every-one must ask himself, "What is my aim?" Yes. People are coming, running to London, running to France, to Germany, to every European country—running. For what? What is the purpose? For what are you coming? *You must know!*

You may say, "I am coming to this country because I am a strong be-liever and I am showing Islam to these unbelievers, so that they may see the light of Islam on my forehead, so that they may be affected by my faith." Are you saying this, or have you come here to take the rubbish of *dunya*, of this world's life?

For all of us, He knows what is in our hearts. You may say something with your lips but He knows what is in our hearts, what is our intention. If we are coming here for the sake of Islam, it is all right. Otherwise, it is difficult; then these countries' darkness is coming on you—darkness, dark clouds, coming and making the sun of your faith under a cloud, and you can't taste the sweetness, the freshness, of faith.

Therefore, everyone must be very careful; yes. Here or there, everyone must know for what we are created, and we must give more time for worshipping our Lord, Almighty Allah. And also you must be like shining stars in the skies, not on earth. People should find in you the stars of Islam, not saying, "From where have those people come? They can go away," writing on walls, "Go away! Go! Go!"

One more Ramadan has just passed away, and we are on our way toward Allah Almighty. Be ready to face His Judgment Day, His glorious Throne. There, you are going to be asked about everything. And we are asking forgiveness—for you, for me, for everyone. ▲

29: choosing the safe way

In this talk, Shaykh Nazim addresses a gathering of English men and women who are interested in spirituality.

You can't remember it, but it is a reality that we were in the Heavens and then we came here for a while, for a very short while. One hundred years ago none of our group was present and after one hundred years none of us will be on earth; perhaps only that little one, a child of two, is then going to be 105. But I am seeing that there is no more time for mankind on this planet.

We haven't any authority to speak on behalf of our own opinions, but according to holy books we may speak. Not from ourselves, but all holy books speak of a last day for this planet, and science also can say that every moving thing must one day come to a stop—*every* moving thing, and we are moving. Therefore, even if we do not look at our holy books, science says that there must come some time when this our planet is going little by little to be tired of turning and moving, and that there must be something to end it.

But we are believers in the holy books that the Lord of the worlds has sent us and in what they say. From beginning up to end, so many prophets, 124,000 prophets at various times and in various countries, have come. They never met with each other in an assembly to make an agreement that when we come to people we must say this or that, but they came over thousands and thousands of years. In each country you can find prophets, and they came to proclaim the same principles of belief, so that we can't say that they are saying something with no reality. It *must* be something true because all of them have said that a day will come to this planet when life is going to stop, when everything is going to stop, and then the Last Day will come.

They have said this and we believe it. There is nothing to object to in it because we haven't any proof for objecting, for rejecting what they are saying. "Perhaps it *may* come," we can say, but we can't say that it is impossible. But in our time, it is a new fashion for people to be atheists, rejecting every belief. But they are wrong, totally wrong people.

There was a famous Muslim philosopher who is well-known in Western countries, also, Ibn Sina, Avicenna. He was a philosopher, trying to put spiritual knowledge side by side with intellectual knowledge—to do it in such a way that people could benefit, not quickly rejecting everything. In our time they are calling it 'positive knowledge'. It is something that you can observe or you can test, and then scientists build knowledge on that base, observing and then testing all the knowledge that scientists or scholars or learned people are so proud of in our time.

Once a scholar, a big scholar, so proud of his knowledge, was sitting like this on a chair and saying to people, "O people, you can ask me anything, as you like. I am ready to answer." Then someone, like this young boy, said, "O my master, I have one question. How many hairs do you have in your beard?"

Who knows how many? You know how many hairs you have here, how many teeth you have? He did not know. So many people whom I am asking don't know even how many teeth they have. How can a person know everything if he is ignorant about himself, about herself? So many people still do not know what is inside themselves. Where are your lungs, your liver? Where are your kidneys? So many people don't know.

That is easy, simple, but that boy asked how many hairs were in his beard, and that scholar was astonished, not knowing what is the answer. And then another one asked, "In an ant, where are the intestines—in the first or the second half of its body?" And he had never seen in books where such knowledge was to be found.

Yes. One cannot know everything. In our time, people are proud of their knowledge and they are trying to produce thousands and thousands of books, but I don't think that anyone is able to keep all knowledge in his head. Never! It is impossible.

And we have, also, a kind of knowledge coming through traditions. You can't reject it. Although we have never seen such things, we are accepting that they *could* happen. And historical events, also—thousands, millions, of events have passed away, and those have come to our knowledge through traditional sources. How can you reject them? Perhaps so many astonishing events may have taken place that do not happen in our days, so many miracles, coming to us through traditions. But even if they do not happen in our days, why are we rejecting them?

And that philosopher, Avicenna, was saying, "O people, if there comes to your ears something that you have never heard of before, even if it is not an accustomed thing to you, even if it is such an unexpected or extraordinary happening, don't be in a rush to reject it. Even if you are not going to accept it easily, you must not be in a hurry to reject it because, if you say that to accept something without asking for evidence is a kind of foolishness, to reject it without evidence is also foolishness." And we are asking, "With what evidence can people reject the possibility that there may be a last day for this world?" *No evidence!* Instead, science can say that it is going to be finished one day, even the sun. Therefore, we are believers.

I saw just now when I was coming a big sign on a building, with writing on it, "SAFEWAY". It affected my heart, and I am asking if people now are on the Safe Way or not. What that building was I don't know. A supermarket? I was thinking that it must be a church, a chapel, a synagogue or such a thing, writing "SAFEWAY" on it. A supermarket? But the meaning is very good.

Everyone must choose the Safe Way for his life, and the Safe Way is to believe—to believe in *something*, because beliefs never harm people, but without beliefs people are going to be harmed.

Once some seven or eight young people came to me. Since we are religious people, they always like to discuss about God; they are trained to be always in opposition to religious people—the new fashion now in our countries, also. Therefore, they came to me and asked, "O shaykh, Shaykh Nazim, do you believe in Paradise and Hell and so on?"

"Yes," I said. "I believe."

"You have proof?"

"Yes, I have proof. But you will not accept my proof, because we have *traditional* proofs from the beginning up to the end. If you accept traditions as knowledge, we believe in that. And if you reject them, then you must reject the whole history of mankind which has come through traditions."

Then they said, "But we are in doubt."

"You may be in doubt, but you can't reject it. And I am asking you to take a Safe Way for your life.

"Now, I will put a glass of milk here to drink and you sit here. Then, when I have put it here, someone comes running and says to me, 'O shaykh, don't put this milk there for those people to drink because the one who brought it to you took a snake out of it.' Then would you drink from this milk?" I asked them.

They said, "No."

"Why wouldn't you drink it? It is milk, and you didn't see that snake taken out of it. Why wouldn't you drink, why would you believe that person? Perhaps, after you, he will come to drink all of it, playing a trick on you. Why would you believe it?"

"Perhaps it may be true. Therefore, the safe way is not to drink."

If you are accepting this, what is the Safe Way? So many sources, traditional sources, speak about the Last Day, about the Resurrection, about Judgment Day, about Paradise, about Hells. What is the evidence for rejecting that? And so many people are accepting it and believing. What is the matter with you to reject it?

If it is correct, then it doesn't matter. We will not lose anything. Are our believers any different in their lives from unbelievers? Yes, we can find some differences, because, although our physical life is the same as theirs, in our inner life we are happy while they are unhappy, because we believe in eternal life.

Day by day I am more happy on behalf of myself. Now one year has passed since we last met here, and a day is coming, quickly, when the whole of life will finish, will end. But I am not displeased or sorry that my life is each day approaching nearer to its end because I believe that that end is going to be a new beginning and I am happy. I am not sorry to see my beard getting whiter each day, no, I am happy. But those people, they are not happy. Unbelievers, for what are they going to be happy? If it is a young person, tomorrow he is going to lose something of his youth—to be down, a little bit, a little bit, a little bit more down; not going up, coming down. And we are giving ourselves the most difficult punishment: to make ourselves hopeless of eternal life.

If we believe, we are happy; if not believing, we are putting that punishment on ourselves. If we believe in the Last Day, does that do some harm to our physical bodies? No; instead, happiness and hope give more strength to believers. They are able to taste well from everything, from every kind of favor in this world. A believer may guard his eyes through his beliefs; his tongue, his ears, his stomach, his heart, every part of his body is going to be excellent, never getting a complaint. And so many saints in Christianity and in Islam who reached real faith, their physical bodies served them throughout their lives, and after death so many of them may be found as they were buried.

Once I was in Sham [Damascus]. There the government was opening a motorway in a place where a saint was buried, and they had to take away that grave. He was a grand-*wali*, a grandshaykh, a great saint. After five hundred years his body was going to be taken out of the ground, and people gathered to look at him when the grave was opened.

I was there because he was a shaykh of *tariqat.* Our Grandshaykh, Shaykh 'Abdullah, had been there seven years in seclusion, and I was invited to be there while the ceremony was going on.

When they opened the grave, a very beautiful scent came from it. And ten days later, I was again passing by that place where his grave had been. Little boys were going down and taking out earth, bringing it to me so I could smell it. A sweet scent like roses was there.

They opened the grave and his body was there in its shroud, and I saw that his long beard, on his chest, had more black hairs than mine, five hundred years after he had been put there. And so many saints, or all saints, are alive in the same condition, here and There.

It is an unbelievable thing, but you can see it. And therefore, believers are on the Safe Way, while unbelievers are punishing themselves. And we are saying, "O our friend, you are free to believe or not to believe, but you are punishing yourself."

We are saying, "Believe in your Lord. Then you can be a good person, because one who believes in his Lord feels responsibility for himself." But that new generation which has come, it does not care about any responsibility—*you* know, in *your* country. More freedom, more freedom, more freedom means that they do not want responsibility in front of anyone, here or Hereafter. Leave aside the Hereafter, they mean to say that we don't want to have any responsibility *here* because responsibility takes us away from freedom. When we are free for everything, it means that we do not have any responsibility.

No-responsibility creatures are in the jungle, not living in a city; no. Whoever lives among people must carry responsibility here. But to feel responsibility only here, now, is not enough to make a person a good one because sometimes people are doing evil hiddenly, justice never reaching them. But the one who believes that his Lord is looking at him wherever he goes, that He is with him, feels more responsibility.

Anyone who believes in his Lord must believe in responsibility, and whoever believes in responsibility must try to carry it in a good way, not leaving it. Therefore, all the prophets came and informed people that there is a Lord and there is a Judgment Day. These two pillars of belief have never changed from the beginning up to the end, and that is in our holy books, coming to us traditionally.

Therefore I said that I don't think that after perhaps one hundred years there may be anyone on earth, even of those who are born ten years, twenty years, fifty years from this time, or that there will be one hundred years more of the period of this life, the Last Day is so near. As Jesus Christ also said, "The Last Day and I are as close to each other as these two fingers, the time was so near when I came," and two thousand years and more have passed since Jesus Christ. And the Last Prophet, Muhammad, the Seal of the Prophets, peace be upon them all, said, "I have come at that time in the day of the life of mankind on earth that, if you say it began with the dawn of Adam, when he came on earth, and went on up to evening time, I have been sent at 'Asr time."[136]

Therefore, the day of mankind which is appointed for our meeting in this life is approaching its end, and we are observing each day so many signs, about which we have been informed through holy books or through traditions that it is approaching. And that is Armageddon, about which it is also written in the Old Testament, the New Testament and the Holy Qur'an that it should be soon, and so many people will pass away. And after that there should come, also, a period, a short period, when this world is going to be renewed or rebuilt.

In our time, people are mostly interested in their physical lives, not interested in their spiritual lives; people are running, going, coming, for only their physical bodies' pleasures or their minds' pleasures. Very, very, very, very, *very* few people are interested in the spiritual life and spiritual pleasures. But physical pleasures, from the first to the second, are always going to be less, while if anyone tastes spiritual pleasures, they are going to increase each day. And I am feeling that this year there is more pleasure spiritually among our attenders. I am feeling that in myself, also; spiritual pleas-

---

[136]That is, during the late afternoon of the life of mankind on earth.

ures are increasing and physical pleasures are becoming less.

And after this Armageddon, people will come to fill this world more than it is full now. People or governments are worrying about population, thinking of enforcing birth control because there are too many people on this planet; they are too afraid, our scientists and governments, saying, "You must have birth control." They are imagining that people are coming to this life by their orders, and by their orders are going away.

That is a new kind of foolishness, to make a "control" on birth. No one can control it except the Creator, the Lord of the worlds. Then, if it is now five billion, at that time, after Armageddon, so many people will go away, and this world is going to be empty, as it was one thousand years ago. How many people were living at that time, one thousand years ago? Now, after Armageddon, it is going to be such an empty world. And then the Lord will send so many of His servants. People will have so many children that it is going to be twice as many as this and everyone is going to be happy.

Those people, all of them, will work for their spiritual lives. They will give only a little time for their physical bodies, and it is going to be enough for them. Enough pleasure, also; if they taste only one piece of food, it will give them as much pleasure as eating a whole lamb; if drinking a little potful, it may give them more pleasure than drinking big jugs. Everything at that time is going to be in a spiritual way, through spiritual powers. If you want to go from here to Scotland, it will be possible to go in a moment from here to Scotland, or farther away.

It is possible. You must not say, "No, it is impossible." You haven't any evidence for rejecting it. One hundred years ago no one accepted or believed that a person could go from England to America in three hours; they would have said, "How can it be?" But it *is* going to be now, and that spiritual power is more than those Concorde's flights' power. At that time, people are going to be persons of divine attributes. Now most people have technical characteristics, making them to be more tied to the earth, but in that time, when we believe that Jesus Christ will come, also, these ties will be cut from our feet, making us rise to the Heavens.

As our holy books are informing and proclaiming, those days are approaching now, quickly, and I myself hope to reach and to see that time, that period. What about all of you? All of you we hope will *insha'Allah* reach those days, those happy days. Now people are living through unhappy days, but those are going to be happy days for everyone who may reach that time. And thank you for listening, for your attention. ▲

Glossary

'Abd-Allah – slave or servant of Allah.

Adab – good manners.

Ahli Sunnah – People of the Prophet's *Sunnah* or Traditions.

Akhirah – the Hereafter.

Al-Fateha – the opening chapter *(surah)* of the Qur'an.

Alhamdulillah *(al-hamdu lil-Lah)* – the praise is for Allah.

'Alim – scholar, learned person.

Allahu Akbar – the *takbir*, meaning, "God is Most Great."

Amanat (amanah) – a trust, something held in trust for another.

'Arif (pl. 'Arifin) – knower; 'Arifin bil-Lah – the knowers of Allah.

Ar-Rahman – the Most Merciful/Compassionate/Munificent and Merciful/Beneficent, the chief of Allah's Holy Names or attributes.

Ar-Rahim – the Most Munificent/Compassionate and Mercy-Giving, another Holy Name, closely connected in meaning to *ar-Rahman*.

As-salamu 'alaikum – "Peace be upon you," the Islamic greeting.

Ashshadu an la ilaha illa-Llah, wa ash-hadu anna Muhammadan 'abduhu wa rasulihu – I bear witness that there is no deity except Allah, and I bear witness that Muhammad is His servant and messenger.

Asmullahu-l-Husna – the ninety-nine excellent or beautiful Names of Allah, which describe His exalted attributes.

'Asr – afternoon; specifically, the third prayer of the day, observed in the latter part of the afternoon.

'Alayhi-s-salam – "peace be on him," represented by the symbol ﷺ.

Astaghfirullah – I seek Allah's forgiveness.

Awliya-Llah – plural of *wali*, a "friend" of Allah, i.e., Muslim saints.

Barakah – blessings.

Batil – false.

Bismillahi-r-Rahmani-r-Rahim – In the name of Allah, the Compassionate, the Merciful, the invocation with which all a Muslim's actions are supposed to begin.

Buraq – the heavenly steed that carried the Prophet during his miraculous Night Journey and Ascension *(al-Isra wal-Me'raj)*.

Dajjal (plural, **dajjalin**) – the False Messiah or Anti-Christ, a fearsome imposter who will appear during the End-Time of this world, producing many supernatural signs and causing people to deviate from the right path, as foretold in numerous *hadiths*.

Da'wa – call, invitation, specifically, to Islam.

Dhalim (plural, **dhalimin**) – those who commit cruelty, injustice, wrong-doing, oppression.

Dhulm (zulm) – cruelty, injustice, oppression, wrong-doing, tyranny, transgressing proper limits.

Du'a – supplication.

Dunya – the earth, this world, this world's life.

'Eid – festival. **'Eid al-Fitr** – the Festival of Fast-Breaking at the end of Ramadan; **'Eid al-Adha** – the Festival of Sacrifice at the time of the *Hajj* (pilgrimage).

Fard – obligatory.

Fasad – evil, mischief, depravity, wickedness, dissension.

Fitrah – natural disposition, temperament, nature; **Fitrat al-Islam** – the nature or innate character of Islam.

Ghusl – the major ablution, consisting of a shower during which water reaches every part of the body.

Grandshaykh – generally, a *wali* of great stature; specifically, Grandshaykh 'Abdullah ad-Daghestani, Shaykh Nazim's shaykh, to whom he was closely attached for forty years up to the time of Grandshaykh's death in 1973.

Hadith (plural, **ahadith**) – reports of the Holy Prophet's sayings, contained in the collections of early *hadith* scholars.

Hajj – pilgrimage to Mecca, the fifth "Pillar" or obligatory worship in Islam

Haqq – truth, reality.

Halal – permissible, lawful, allowed.

Haram – prohibited, unlawful, forbidden.

Hasha – Never! God forbid!

Hatif – the divine Voice of inspiration.

Hazretleri – the Turkish equivalent of "His Holiness."

Hijrah – the Prophet's emigration from Mecca to Medina in the year 622. The Islamic *(Hijri)* calendar begins from this date.

Imam – generally, leader; specifically, the leader of a congregational prayer.

Iman – faith, belief.

Injil – the original scripture revealed to the prophet Jesus.

Insha'Allah – if Allah wills.

'Isha – evening; specifically, the fifth prayer of the day, observed at night.

Ism al-A'dham – the greatest of the Beautiful Names of Allah.

Istighfar – seeking forgiveness.

Jahiliyyah – generally, ignorance; specifically, ignorance of the divinely-revealed guidance.

Jihad – strenuous effort or striving, whether by force of arms, in self-defense by the tongue or pen, or within one's inner self.

Jum'a – Friday; **Jum'a khutbah** – the sermon of the weekly Friday congregational prayer.

Kalimat ash-Shahadah – the Word of Witnessing or Proclamation of Faith, *Ashshadu an la ilaha illa-Llah, wa ashhadu anna Muhammadan 'abduhu wa rasulihu.*

Khalifah – deputy, successor, vice-gerent.

Kufr – disbelief or unbelief, denial, ingratitude.

La ilaha illa-Llah, Muhammadu Rasul-

Allah – There is no deity except Allah, Muhammad is Allah's Messenger.

Lailat al-Bara'at – the Night of Absolution, during which, according to Islamic belief, the year's accounting of a person's deeds and sustenance are examined, and those who have led righteous lives are granted divine forgiveness. It is observed on the night between the 14th and 15th of the month of Sha'ban.

Lailat al-Isra wal Me'raj – the Night of the Journey and Ascension of the Holy Prophet, observed on the night between the 26th and 27th of the month of Rajab.

Lailat al-Maulid – the Prophet's birthnight, observed on the night between the 11th and 12th of the month of Rabi' al-Awwal.

Lailat al-Me'raj – the Night of the Holy Prophet's Ascension (see *Lailat al-Isra wal Me'raj*).

Lailat al-Qadr – the Night of Power, during which the angel Gabriel brought the first revelation of the Qur'an to the Prophet in the year 610 C.E. Its anniversary is commemorated on one of the odd-numbered nights of the last ten days of Ramadan.

Madhhab – school of Islamic jurisprudence *(fiqh)*.

Mahgrib – sunset; the occident or West; the fourth prayer of the day, observed at sunset.

Mahshar – the plain of the gathering of the Day of Resurrection, in the vicinity of Damascus.

Maqam – station, position.

Ma'rifat – divine knowledge; **ma'rifat-Allah** – knowledge of Allah.

Masjid – mosque.

Minbar – pulpit from which sermons are delivered.

Muhammadu Rasul-Allah – Muhammad is the Messenger of Allah.

Mumin – believer.

Murid – disciple, follower.

Murshid – a guide, instructor or director; in a more specific sense, a spiritual guide or teacher, or the head of a religious order.

Nafs – lower self, ego.

Nur – light.

Qiblah – direction; specifically, the direction of Mecca faced by Muslims in every part of the globe.

Rak'at/Rak'ah – a cycle or unit of the Islamic prayer *(salat* or *namaz)*, which is repeated a given number of times in each segment of the five daily prayers.

Ramadan – the ninth month of the Islamic calendar, the month of fasting.

Rasul-Allah – Messenger of Allah.

Rizq – provision, livelihood, sustenance.

Sabr – patience, endurance, steadfastness; **sabirin** – those who have the quality of *sabr.*

Sahabah (singular, **sahabi**) – Companions of the Prophet.

Sajdah (sujud) – prostration.

Salam – greeting, specifically, the Islamic greeting, *"As-salamu 'alaikum,* peace be upon you."

Salat/Salah – the Islamic prayer.

Salla-Llahu 'alayhi wa sallam – Allah's peace and blessings be upon him (the Prophet), represented by the symbol ﷺ.

Sayyid – master; **Sayyidina** – our master.

Shahadah – witnessing, the Islamic proclamation of faith.

Shari'at/Shari'ah – literally, way; a divine law; specifically, the canonical law of Islam..

Shaykh/Sheikh – an old man, elder, head of a family or tribe; a teacher, preacher or scholar; the head of a *tariqah* or Sufi order.

Sohbet – talk, lecture.

Subhanallah – glory be to Allah.

Sultan – ruler, monarch.

Sunnah – the practices or traditions of the Holy Prophet; that is, what he did, said, recommended or approved of in his Companions.

Surah – chapter of the Qur'an.

Taharah – cleanliness, purification.

Tarawih – the special night prayers of Ramadan, observed after *Isha*, the night prayer.

Tariqat/Tariqah – literally, way, road or path; specifically, an Islamic religious order or path of discipline and devotion under a guide or sheikh, i.e., Islamic Sufism.

Tasawwuf – Sufism.

Taurat – the original Torah revealed by Allah to Moses 🕊.

Tuba – happiness, felicity.

'Ulama – plural of *'alim*.

Ummah – nation, faith community.

Wali – friend, patron; in the specific sense used in this book, a Muslim saint; **Wali-Ullah** – a friend of Allah, i.e., a Muslim saint.

Wa min Allah at-tawfiq – And the success is from Allah.

Wudu – ablution for prayers..

Ya Rabb – O Lord; **Ya Rabbi** – O my Lord.

Other titles from

Islamic Supreme Council of America

Online ordering available from www.Amazon.com

The Path to Spiritual Excellence
By Shaykh Muhammad Nazim Adil al-Haqqani
ISBN 1-930409-18-4, Paperback. 180 pp.

This compact volume provides practical steps to purify the heart and overcome the destructive characteristics that deprive us of peace and inner satisfaction. On this amazing journey doubt, fear, and other negative influences that plague our lives - and which we often pass on to our children - can be forever put aside. Simply by introducing in our daily lives those positive thought patterns and actions that attract divine support, we can reach spiritual levels that were previously inaccessible.

In the Mystic Footsteps of Saints
By Shaykh Muhammad Nazim Adil al-Haqqani
Volume 1 - ISBN 1-930409-05-2
Volume 2 - ISBN 1-930409-09-5
Volume 3 - ISBN 1-930409-13-3, Paperback. Ave. length 200 pp.

Narrated in a charming, old-world storytelling style, this highly spiritual series offers several volumes of practical guidance on how to establish serenity and peace in daily life, heal emotional and spiritual scars, and discover the role we are each destined to play in the universal scheme.

Classical Islam and the Naqshbandi Sufi Tradition

By Shaykh Muhammad Hisham Kabbani

ISBN 1-930409-23-0, Hardback. 950 pp.

ISBN 1-930409-10-9, Paperback. 744 pp.

This esteemed work includes an unprecedented historical narrative of the forty saints of the renowned Naqshbandi Golden Chain, dating back to Prophet Muhammad in the early seventh century. With close personal ties to the most recent saints, the author has painstakingly compiled rare accounts of their miracles, disciplines, and how they have lent spiritual support throughout the world for fifteen centuries. Traditional Islam and the Naqshbandi Sufi Tradition is a shining tribute to developing human relations at the highest level, and the power of spirituality to uplift humanity from its lower nature to that of spiritual triumph.

The Naqshbandi Sufi Tradition

Guidebook of Daily Practices and Devotions

By Shaykh Muhammad Hisham Kabbani

ISBN 1-930409-22-2, Paperback. 352 pp.

This book details the spiritual practices which have enabled devout seekers to awaken certainty of belief and to attain stations of nearness to the Divine Presence. The Naqshbandi Devotions are a source of light and energy, an oasis in a worldly desert. Through the manifestations of Divine Blessings bestowed on the practitioners of these magnificent rites, they will be granted the power of magnanimous healing, by which they seek to cure the hearts of mankind darkened by the gloom of spiritual poverty and materialism.

This detailed compilation, in English, Arabic and transliteration, includes the daily personal dhikr as well as the rites performed with every obligatory prayer, rites for holy days and details of the pilgrimage to Mecca and the visit of Prophet Muhammad in Madinah.

Naqshbandi Awrad
of Mawlana Shaykh Muhammad Nazim Adil al-Haqqani
Compiled by Shaykh Muhammad Hisham Kabbani
ISBN 1-930409-06-0, Paperback. 104 pp.

This book presents in detail, in both English, Arabic and transliteration, the daily, weekly and date-specific devotional rites of Naqshbandi practitioners, as prescribed by the world guide of the Naqshbandi-Haqqani Sufi Order, Mawlana Shaykh Muhammad Nazim Adil al-Haqqani.

Pearls and Coral, I & II
By Shaykh Muhammad Hisham Kabbani
ISBN 1-930409-07-9, Paperback. 220 pp.
ISBN 1-930409-08-7, Paperback. 220 pp.

A series of lectures on the unique teachings of the Naqshbandi Order, originating in the Near East and Central Asia, which has been highly influential in determining the course of human history in these regions. Always pushing aspirants on the path of Gnosis to seek higher stations of nearness to the God, the Naqshbandi Masters of Wisdom melded practical methods with deep spiritual wisdom to build an unequalled methodology of ascension to the Divine Presence.

The Sufi Science of Self-Realization
A Guide to the Seventeen Ruinous Traits, the Ten Steps to Discipleship and the Six Realities of the Heart
By Shaykh Muhammad Hisham Kabbani
ISBN 1-930409-29-X, Paperback. 244 pp.

The path from submersion in the negative traits to the unveiling of these six powers is known as migration to Perfected Character. Through a ten-step program, the author--a master of the Naqshbandi Sufi Path--describes the science of eliminating the seventeen ruinous characteristics of the tyrannical ego, to achieve purification of the soul. The sincere seeker who follows these steps, with devotion and discipline, will acheive an unveiling of the six powers which lie dormant within every human heart.

Encyclopedia of Islamic Doctrine
Shaykh Muhammad Hisham Kabbani
ISBN: 1-871031-86-9, Paperback, Vol. 1-7.

The most comprehensive treatise on Islamic belief in the English language. The only work of its kind in English, Shaykh Hisham Kabbani's seven volume Encyclopedia of Islamic Doctrine is a monumental work covering in great detail the subtle points of Islamic belief and practice. Based on the four canonical schools of thought, this is an excellent and vital resource to anyone seriously interested in spirituality. There is no doubt that in retrospect, this will be the most significant work of this age.

The Approach of Armageddon?
An Islamic Perspective
by Shaykh Muhammad Hisham Kabbani
ISBN 1-930409-20-6, Paperback 292 pp.

This unprecedented work is a "must read" for religious scholars and laypersons interested in broadening their understanding of centuries-old religious traditions pertaining to the Last Days. This book chronicles scientific breakthroughs and world events of the Last Days as foretold by Prophet Muhammad. Also included are often concealed ancient predictions of Islam regarding the appearance of the anti-Christ, Armageddon, the leadership of believers by Mahdi ("the Savior"), the second coming of Jesus Christ, and the tribulations preceding the Day of Judgment. We are given final hope of a time on earth filled with peace, reconciliation, and prosperity; an age in which enmity and wars will end, while wealth is overflowing. No person shall be in need and the entire focus of life will be spirituality."

Keys to the Divine Kingdom
By Shaykh Muhammad Hisham Kabbani
ISBN 1-930409-28-1, Paperback. 140 pp.

God said, "We have created everything in pairs." This has to do with reality versus imitation. Our physical form here in this earthly life is only a reflection of our heavenly form. Like plastic fruit and real fruit, one is real, while the other is an imitation. This book looks at the nature of the physical world, the laws governing the universe and from this starting point, jumps into the realm of spiritual knowledge - Sufi teachings which must be "tasted" as opposed to read or spoken. It will serve to open up to the reader the mystical path of saints which takes human beings from the world of forms and senses to the world within the heart, the world of gnosis and spirituality - a world filled with wonders and blessings.

My Little Lore of Light
By Hajjah Amina Adil
ISBN 1-930409-35-4, Paperback, 204 pp.

A children's version of Hajjah Amina Adil's four volume work, *Lore Of Light*, this books relates the stories of God's prophets, from Adam to Muhammad, upon whom be peace, drawn from traditional Ottoman sources. This book is intended to be read aloud to young children and to be read by older children for themselves. The stories are shortened and simplified but not changed. The intention is to introduce young children to their prophets and to encourage thought and discussion in the family about the eternal wisdom these stories embody.

Muhammad: The Messenger of Islam
His Life and Prophecy
By Hajjah Amina Adil
ISBN 1-930409-11-7, Paperback. 608 pp.

Since the 7th century, the sacred biography of Islam's Prophet Muhammad has shaped the perception of the religion and its place in world history. This book skilfully etches the personal portrait of a man of incomparable moral and spiritual stature, as seen through the eyes of Muslims around the world. Compiled from classical Ottoman Turkish sources and translated into English, this comprehensive biography is deeply rooted in the life example of its prophet.

The Practice of Sufi Meditation
and the Healing Power of Divine Energy
By Dr. Hedieh Mirahmadi and Sayyid Nurjan Mirahmadi
ISBN: 1-930409-26-5, Paperback. 100 pp.

For those who have reached a level of understanding of the illusory nature of the world around us and seek to discern the reality that lies behind it, Sufi meditation

- *muraqabah* - is the doorway through which we can pass from this realm of delusion into the realm of realities.

This book presents the spiritual background behind the practice of Sufi meditation, then takes the reader step-by-step, through the basics of spiritual connection based on the ancient teachings of the Naqshbandi Sufi masters of Central Asia.

The Honor of Women in Islam
By Professor Yusuf da Costa
ISBN 1-930409-06-0, Paperback. 104 pp.

Relying on Islamic source texts, this concise, scholarly work elucidates the true respect and love for women inherent in the Islamic faith. It examines the pre-Islamic state of women, highlights the unprecedented rights they received under Islamic Law, and addresses the prominent beliefs and prevailing cultures throughout the Muslim world regarding the roles of women in familial, social service and community development, business, academic, religious, and even judicial circles. In addition, brief case studies of historical figures such as Mary, mother of Jesus are presented within the Islamic tradition.